Styles of Extinction: Cormac McCarthy's *The Road*

Styles of Extinction: Cormac McCarthy's *The Road*

Edited by

*Julian Murphet
and Mark Steven*

continuum

Continuum International Publishing Group

The Tower Building
11 York Road
London
SE1 7NX

80 Maiden Lane
Suite 704
New York
NY 10038

www.continuumbooks.com

© Julian Murphet and Mark Steven 2012

ISBN: HB: 978-1-4411-6934-1
PB: 978-1-4411-8505-1

Library of Congress Cataloging-in-Publication Data
Styles of extinction : Cormac McCarthy's The road / [edited] by Julian Murphet and Mark Steven.
pages cm
Includes bibliographical references and index.
ISBN-13: 978-1-4411-6934-1 (hardcover)
ISBN-10: 1-4411-6934-2 (hardcover)
ISBN-13: 978-1-4411-8505-1 (pbk.)
ISBN-10: 1-4411-8505-4 (pbk.)
1. McCarthy, Cormac, 1933- Road. 2. Fathers and sons in literature. 3. Good and evil in literature. 4. Apocalypse in literature. 5. Regression (Civilization) in literature. 6. Survival in literature. 7. Redemption in literature. I. Murphet, Julian. II. Steven, Mark.

PS3563.C337R6337 2012
813'.54—dc23

2011050828

Typeset by Deanta Global Publishing Services, Chennai, India
Printed and bound in the United States of America

CONTENTS

A NOTE ON THE TEXTS

All page references to Cormac McCarthy's *The Road* (2006) will be included parenthetically within the text of each chapter. They refer to the Picador paperback edition, first published in 2007.

1

Introduction: "The charred ruins of a library"

MARK STEVEN AND JULIAN MURPHET

Is the book really, as many contemporary soothsayers would have it, in its death throes as a medium? Its five hundred years of unparalleled success—monopoly, even—in the storage and dissemination of information over, has the codex come up against its own irreversible extinction? Walter Benjamin was already thinking something of this sort when, in 1931, he contemplated the image of his personal library sealed up in multiple wooden crates. There he foretold the end of personal libraries assembled by literary subjects. "I do know that night is coming for the type that I am discussing here," he writes: "But, as Hegel put it, only when it is dark does the owl of Minerva begin its flight. Only in extinction is the collector comprehended."[1] If a personal library is the physiognomy of its collector's soul, if it gives material body to a spirit shaped by literature, then the passing of its time on earth will surely have altered the face of the world itself—to that extent a less soulful, a more dispirited place. But in that final darkling passage of the Hegelian owl over the extinguished fire of "man," something like a full and final comprehension of its grandeur will at last come to light, before twinkling out altogether.

The library we come across in Cormac McCarthy's novel, *The Road*, attests to an extinction having befallen both the books and the spirit to which those books corresponded:

Years later he'd stood in the charred ruins of a library where blackened books lay in pools of water. Shelves tipped over. Some rage at the lies arranged in their thousands row on row. He picked up one of the books and thumbed through the heavy bloated pages. He'd not have thought the value of the smallest thing predicated on a world to come. It surprised him. That the space which these things occupied was itself an expectation. He let the book fall and took a last look around and made his way out into the cold gray light. (199)

The books arranged here betray their serially broken promise. In their "heavy bloated pages," they have been reduced to lumpish materiality, body without spirit, the latter of which seems to have taken flight along with Minerva's owl: "a world to come," "an expectation," an extraterritorial, utopian no-place that is irreducible to the matter on which it is predicated. Literature, that seemingly inexhaustible intra referential system of dream, fantasy, illusion, projection, imprecation, beatification, imagination, and fancy, here subjected to an anonymous collective rage at such gargantuan betrayal, and left blackened and saturated; a guilty pulp fiction.

The recasting of the abstract fecund promise into countless individual "lies" is a literary allusion. From this ruined library, the last book looks back over its shoulder to glimpse what is arguably the first: Cervantes' *Don Quixote*. Recall how that paradigmatic picaresque begins with the assembly of the eponymous hero's library, and note the affective force this library has in the shaping of his spirit. "Everything he read in his books took possession of his imagination," we read:

> enchantments, fights, battles, challenges, wounds, sweet nothings, love affairs, storms and impossible absurdities. The idea that this whole fabric of famous fabrications was real so established itself in his mind that no history of the world was truer for him.[2]

For Cervantes, mere empirical truth is elevated via the intensified "truth" of books to create a wholly literary worldview. It is a worldview that is, by the author's later admission, absolutely and unforgivably false ("my only desire has been to make men hate those false, absurd histories in books of chivalry"[3]). The novel as a form finds its most ardent motivations in precisely this negative desire, this ferocious modernizing will to traduce, invert, explode, and denounce feudal absurdities; and yet this statement of ideological intent only offsets the exuberance that drives the book's narrative, which takes flight from its hero's perfect, self-satisfying immersion in his own well-stocked library.

After Don Quixote's first quest he falls ill, raving mad, so that the town's priest thinks it best to burn the books and to seal off the library:

> One of the remedies that the priest and the barber has prescribed at that time for their friend's malady was to have his library walled up and sealed off so that he couldn't find his books when he got up—maybe if the cause was removed the effect might cease—and to tell him that an enchanter had carried them off, with the library and all; and this was done without delay. Two days later Don Quixote did get up, and his first action was to go and look at his books; and, since he couldn't find the room in which he'd left them, he wandered all over the house searching for it. He kept going up to the place where the door used to be, and feeling for it with his hands, and running his eyes backwards and forwards over the walls without uttering a word . . .[4]

Like the man in *The Road*, Don Quixote turns out to the "cold gray light" and silently continues on his quest. What is different, however, is that in Cervantes' text there is a palpable sense of hope, for the noble picaro has already internalized the library and is driven forward by its lessons no matter how false they might be. It is thus that this first conflagration inspires the epic quest, around which the first book is constructed, and whose final steps are being taken in *The Road*.

Don Quixote's library comprised countless romances and histories of chivalry, which together negatively conditioned the novel's openly critical form. What books can we imagine lining the shelves of the charred library in *The Road*? "There is no prophet in the earth's long chronicle who's not honored here today," we read. "Whatever form you spoke of you were right." (297) If *The Road* has its prophets surely they will be have been lifted from the canon of American prose (Melville, Whitman, Faulkner, Hemingway), from Anglo-Irish poetics (Beckett, Yeats, Eliot), and from European expression (Kafka, Mandelstam, Baudelaire). If these are the books that populate McCarthy's blasted library, then perhaps it will be wise to conjecture on McCarthy's engagement with the project named modernism, of which all of these earlier writers are either influentially prescient or major practitioners.

If McCarthy's novel has any lingering commitment to the modernist masterpieces he alludes to, it is to be discerned at the level of style. Here is David Trotter on modernist form:

> In modernist writing, mimesis is not so much an end in itself as an occasion for the triumph of poesis. Both novelists and poets invoked through their choice of subject matter and technique a resistance to literature which they knew would yield only to the excess literature at their command.[5]

McCarthy's novel lacks the sense of narrative destiny we would otherwise associate with the "quest," and it rejects the cheap thrills of contemporary apocalypse scenarios; but what it most wants to evoke is this very stylistic "signature" of poesis peculiar to modernist letters. This is why John Hillcoat's genuflectingly faithful film adaptation lacked the tremendous energy of its literary source: the book's mimetic narrative was only ever a precursor to its style, which cannot be translated in any simple way into a medium other than prose; to film and project *The Road* is to lose sight of that. "This tendency in modernist theory and practice," Trotter continues, "might be thought of, by analogy with Nietzsche's will-to-power and will-to-life, as a will-to-literature. Modernism was one of the fiercest campaign ever mounted in the favor of literature."[6]

That said, let us add one more library to our collection: the quintessentially modernist one in *Ulysses'* "Scylla and Charybdis":

> Rest suddenly possessed the discreet vaulted cell, rest of warm and brooding air.
>
> A vestal's lamp.
>
> Here he ponders things that were not: what Caesar would have lived to do had he believed the soothsayer: what might have been: possibilities of the possible as possible: things not known: what name Achilles bore when he lived among women.
>
> Coffined thoughts around me, in mummycases, embalmed in spice of words. Thoth, god of libraries, a birdgod, mooncrowned. And I heard the voice of that Egyptian highpriest. *In painted chambers loaded with tilebooks.*

They are still. Once quick in the brains of men. Still: but an itch
of death is in them, to tell me in my ear a maudlin tale, urge me
to wreck their will.[7]

Joyce's library also speaks to its own extinction; and indeed, these
shelves line the walls of a pharaonic tomb. However, what is
remarkable here is the style in which that extinction is reckoned:
death is only the dialectical antithesis to life; from stillness comes
action, and that action is presented here as the "excess" of literature
at the author's command. It is by opening up a space of "things
that were not" that literature fulfills its treacherous promise, and
it opens up that space via the stylization of its form. It creates
unpredictable spaces of what Joyce refers to as "possibilities of the
possible as possible" and what McCarthy's narrator calls "a world
to come." Could it be, then, that *The Road* is a belated addition
to a modernist spirit first energized by Cervantes and reactivated
through Joyce?

Certainly, in a true modernist fashion, the book performs its own
doomed refusal to go gently into the good night of an ordained
extinction, at the level of a stubborn stylistic singularity. It stakes
a claim to literary style as the final, precious barrier between itself
and the void it viscerally conjures up in narrative and imaginary
form. Style flickers like a last taper in the harsh winds blown down
along the soggy library shelves, lighting here and there on some
stray phrase, some lost chronicle of humankind, in order to poach
from them a stubborn force—a subjectivity—that has not yet
succumbed to the general darkness. It works according to a fairly
obvious economy. Page after page of the most minimal sentence
forms—"He froze. He was wrapped in one of the grey blankets
and he would have been hard to see but not impossible. But he
thought probably they had smelled the smoke. They stood talking.
Then they went on. He sat down" (88–9)—as if to indicate a craven
capitulation to the degree zero of American fiction: distaste for the
more complex moods, syntactical simplicity, active voice, rabid
aversion from hypotaxis, a tendency to verbless asyndeton and
parataxis, sourceless anaphora, and an air of "adaptability," like
so many airport novels and bestsellers, as if written with the film
rights uppermost in mind. But among this narrative dictatorialness,
a stray locution, phrase, or simple word occasionally intrudes, as if
to establish a fragile bulwark of resistance: "the corrugate shapes of

old harrowtroughs," (208) "he knelt and laid him in the gritty duff," (123) "like a grave yawning at judgment day in some old apocalyptic painting," (165) "that silent corridor through the drifting ash where they struggled forever in the road's cold coagulate." (204) Yeats' falcon has flown wide and away from the falconer to whom it is only a distant memory, but its gyres still drive the sentences in with it is remembered:

> In that long ago somewhere very near this place he'd watched a falcon fall down the long blue wall of the mountain and break with the keel of its breastbone the midmost from a flight of cranes and take it to the river below all gangly and wrecked and trailing its loose and blowsy plumage in the still autumn air. (19)

And then a whole, isolated paragraph whose overt function is to preserve "style" against the relentless indicative tyranny: "Do you think that your fathers are watching? That they weigh you in their ledgerbook? Against what? There is no book and your fathers are dead in the ground." (209)

The functioning of this stylistic economy is quite clear: style appears amid the routine production of narrative sentences like the fossilized prints of an extinct mammal, left in the baking tar eons ago; calling to mind a "book" that might vouchsafe the legislative authority of those august modernist "fathers" collectively responsible for establishing literature's urgent moral value in a wilderness of prose. And yet never refashioning it as such: this late book is not a "book" in that sense (Mallarmé's *Livre du monde*[8]), and it cannot be. It ploughs an exhausted literary harrowtrough with the dulled equipment of a vanished past; the moments of intensity it gives rise to are the sparks thrown off by that edgeless blade as it strikes the insensible rocks of the present. If it posits a style of extinction (and thus constructs a self-conscious constellation with Beckett and Coetzee), it is one unleavened by that irrefragable quotient of transformativity—of possibility within circumscription—which characterizes all modernisms, even the very late ones. All-too precious in its moments of virtuosity, unable to find a formal solution to the binary oscillation between narrative and style, *The Road* consciously performs the epiphenomenal, inconsequential status of literature's state of exception today: its lapsing from a Borgesian library, full of shimmering and terrifying possibility, into a charred ruin of the same, where nothing remains but the disappointment of that expectation.

If there is a point on which all of the essays in this volume converge, it is that of style—style as what negates, but also as what succumbs to, the entropic horizon of what, inexorably, is. These essays are full of disagreements, and find as much to distrust and question as they do to celebrate and admire in a book so exquisitely positioned on the undecidable formal cusp between postmodern readability and modernist dis-/re-enchantment. Yet they all share an impulse of sober analytic attentiveness, as if every word in the text counted; as if the pages of this book are what they sometimes purport to be—well-nigh sacred, apocalyptic in the true sense of issuing a vision for a community of believers. Attuned to the cultural ironies of this portentous religiosity of a paperback bestseller, the essays assembled here are nonetheless united in their serious dedication to the old-fashioned tasks of close reading and hermeneutics; finding equivocal sustenance in a novel that simultaneously advances and retracts its own literary ambition: two parts zombie picture, one part *Worstward Ho*.

In the first two essays, Chris Danta and Sean Pryor pay careful attention to the question of style as it pertains to the virtually molecular properties of McCarthy's novel. Danta concentrates his analysis on the book's monochromic color palette and Pyror explores the effect of McCarthy's prose rhythms. Both essays contend that these patently formal features of the text are not merely decorative but, rather, they are central to our understanding and assessment of *The Road*; and indeed, the attentive analyses of Danta and Pryor both gesture toward the extensive implications of form as it reacts to the novel's position with literary and cultural history. Grace Hellyer then examines the broadly allegorical dimension of *The Road* with an essay that compares the book's sense of melancholia to the poetics of Charles Baudelaire. She argues that the man's evocation of quasi theological forms is a defense to the suicidal melancholia that engulfed his wife and which threatens the book's entire worldview. The essays by Mark Steven, Paul Sheehan, and Julian Murphet all construct their arguments upon the premise that *The Road* is itself an allegorical text, connecting up its formal and narrative concerns with the panorama of its historical moment. These three essays together explore the political fortunes of McCarthy's book, with each patiently demonstrating how its stylistic victories

might be hard-won indeed and from what it is these victories must
be taken. And finally, Paul Patton's essay engages *The Road* for
its representation of the sublime, arguing that its moral economy
ultimately yields to an "unimaginable" figure of the "overman."

Notes

1 Walter Benjamin, "Unpacking My Library: A Talk about Collecting,"
   in *Selected Writings: 1931–34*, Volume 2, part 2, trans. Harry Zohn,
   eds. M. W. Jennings, Howard Eiland, and Gary Smith (Cambridge
   MA and London: Harvard University Press, 1999), 492.
2 Cervantes, *Don Quixote*, trans. John Rutherford (London and New
   York: Penguin, 2000), 27.
3 Cervantes, *Don Quixote*, 982.
4 Cervantes, *Don Quixote*, 59–60.
5 David Trotter, "The Modernist Novel," in *The Cambridge
   Companion to Modernism*, ed. M. Levenson (Cambridge: Cambridge
   University Press, 1999), 74–5.
6 Trotter, "The Modernist Novel," 74.
7 James Joyce, *Ulysses* (London and New York: Penguin, 2000), 247–8.
8 As Mallarmé wrote to Jules Huret, "tout, au monde, existe pour
   aboutir à un Livre." *Oeuvres completes* (Paris: Gallimard, 1945), 378.

2

"The cold illucid world": The poetics of gray in Cormac McCarthy's *The Road*

CHRIS DANTA

*Grey cloudless sky verge upon verge grey timeless air of
those nor for God nor for his enemies.*

—Samuel Beckett, *Fizzle 8: For to end yet again*

*It seems to me sometimes the earth must have got stuck, in
the heart of winter, in the gray of evening.*

—Samuel Beckett, *Rough for Theatre I*

The gray world

Ludwig Wittgenstein once remarked that "colours are a stimulus to philosophizing."[1] If there is a color in Cormac McCarthy's Pulitzer Prize-winning novel *The Road* that spurs us to philosophize, it is undoubtedly the color gray. On my count, the word *gray* occurs 81 times in this short novel, with the additional permutations *graying*, *grayness*, and *grayblue* each occurring once. It is impossible to read *The Road* without noticing how gray everything looks: days are gray; dusks are gray; dawns are gray; the light and the sky are gray; the landscape is gray; the city is gray; tree stumps are gray; the ash is gray; the slush, sleet, and ice are gray; the beach, sea, and hagmoss are gray; the water is gray; the window is gray; clothes are gray; the human body, both living and dead, is gray; hair is gray; teeth are gray; viscera are gray. And last but not least—the heart is gray.

The post-apocalyptic world of *The Road* has been grayed out—has moved from a brighter to a fainter shade. McCarthy makes this global shift of tone apparent in the novel's very opening sentences: "When he awoke in the woods in the dark and the cold of the night he'd reached out to touch the child sleeping beside him. Nights dark beyond darkness and the days more gray each one than what had gone before. Like the onset of some cold glaucoma dimming away the world" (1). The gently personifying simile of the third sentence is significant: the world is like an eye that is slowly losing its sight. Interestingly, the etymology of *glaucoma* conjures the color gray. A medical condition in which one's sight gradually deteriorates into blindness, *glaucoma* comes from the Greek word *glaukos*, the English equivalent of which is *glaucous*, meaning "Of a dull or pale green colour passing into greyish blue" ("Glaucous").

In *The Road*, McCarthy develops his opening simile of the glaucomatic world into a poetics of vision that takes account of the apocalypse through a grim and almost-biblical cataloguing of the ubiquitous grayness of things. Gray marks the apocalypse in this novel—or, to be more precise, gray marks the sheer fragility of the post-apocalypse, in which everything appears to be heading, like the central figure of the father, inexorably toward its death: "He thought if he lived long enough the world at last would all be lost. Like the dying world the newly blind inhabit, all of it slowly fading from memory" (17).

Perhaps the chief rhetorical gesture of the post-apocalyptic text is to conflate being with event. The apocalyptic event that precedes and gives impetus to the post-apocalyptic narrative penetrates into the very being of things so as to alter them irrevocably. Significantly, I think, the event that so restructures the being of the things of the world in *The Road* features a long shear of light: "The clocks stopped at 1:17. A long shear of light and then a series of low concussions" (54). Like so many other things in this novel the disaster remains unnamed. In fact, so spare is McCarthy's style in *The Road* that the words *disaster, catastrophe,* and *apocalypse* never appear. Critics have wondered whether his precise but incomplete description of the event refers to a nuclear apocalypse or to some other natural cataclysm. My own sense is that McCarthy is more concerned to trace the consequences than he is to identify the cause of the catastrophe. As Richard Gray puts it, "The unnameable remains unnamed, except in its human consequences."[2] According to the poetics of vision that McCarthy develops in *The Road*, what matters is that the world has been overexposed to a destructive form of light. And what we glimpse from the opening sentences of the novel is the main effect of this overexposure: an irreparable loss of luminosity, a dimming away of the world, an ecological glaucoma.

The gray and glaucomatic world of *The Road* recalls the gray and glaucomatic world of another well-known post-apocalyptic text: namely, Samuel Beckett's *Endgame* (1958). Beckett's play begins with the stage directions: "*Bare interior. Grey light.*"[3] When the servile Clov climbs up a ladder to take a look out one of the two small windows in the room with a telescope it becomes apparent that this gray light is the after-effect of some kind of global catastrophe. The landscape Clov describes to his blind and wheelchair-bound master Hamm has been grayed out like that of *The Road*. "All is . . . Corpsed," he says. "The light is sunk."[4] Somewhat dismayed by this description, Hamm then presses Clov for the whereabouts of the sun.

HAMM: And the sun?
CLOV: (*looking.*) Zero.
HAMM: But it should be sinking. Look again.
CLOV: (*looking.*) Damn the sun.
HAMM: Is it night already then?
CLOV: (*looking.*) No.
HAMM: Then what is it?
CLOV: (*looking.*) Grey. (*Lowering the telescope, turning towards HAMM, louder.*) Grey! (*Pause. Still louder.*) GRREY! *Pause. He gets down, approaches HAMM from behind, whispers in his ear.*
HAMM: (*starting.*) Grey! Did I hear you say grey?
CLOV: Light black. From pole to pole.[5]

Where McCarthy offers us a two-sentence description of the disastrous event in *The Road*, Beckett is even more circumspect in *Endgame* and offers nothing whatsoever. But it is easy enough to spot the correspondences between these two post-apocalyptic landscapes. Moreover, it is also possible to detect a similar poetics of vision operating in both works. "When the curtain rises on *Endgame*," writes Hugh Kenner:

> sheets drape all visible objects as in a furniture warehouse. Clov's first act is to uncurtain the two high windows and inspect the universe; his second is to remove the sheets and fold them carefully over his arm, disclosing two ash cans and a figure in an armchair. This is so plainly a metaphor for waking up that we fancy the stage, with its high peepholes, to be the inside of an immense skull.[6]

Clov peering out with his "glass" from a bare interior onto the devastated terrain of *Endgame* thus figures a glaucomatic eye to which everything suddenly appears gray.

As my epigraphs indicate, gray is a quintessentially Beckettian color. Indeed, when Beckett directed his plays himself, he "often spoke 'about gray, a colour gray' that he wanted to dominate the stage."[7] In his 1989 essay "The Writing of the Generic," the French philosopher Alain Badiou identifies gray as the color of the site of being in Beckett. For Badiou, Beckett's fictive world tends toward "a kind of motionless simplicity."[8] And nowhere is this motionless simplicity that suppresses the space of the trajectory better exemplified, Badiou thinks, than in the grayed-out landscape of Beckett's late work *Lessness* (1969): "Grey sky no cloud no sound no stir earth ash grey [*noir grise*] sand. Little body same grey as the earth sky ruins only upright. Ash grey all sides earth sky as one all sides endlessness."[9] Here, it is as if Beckett has shrunk being itself to an impermeable core of "ash grey" (which is Beckett's own translation of his original French phrase *noir grise*). According to Badiou:

> Once its fictive purification is attained, the space of being [in Beckett] . . . could be termed a 'black-grey'. . . . What is the black-grey? It is a black that no light can be supposed to contrast with; it is an un-contrasted black. This black is sufficiently grey that no light can be opposed to it as its Other. Abstractly, the site of

being is fictioned as a black-grey enough to be anti-dialectical, distinct from every contradiction with the light. The black-grey is a black that has to be taken in its own disposition and that forms no pair with anything else. . . .This final and unique site, the anti-dialectical black-grey, does not come within the realm of clear and distinct ideas. The question of being, grasped in its localization, cannot be distinguished or separated out through any ideal articulation.[10]

An important point to grasp here is that gray is a color that marks eventuation or transformation—it is a color that things become, as when we say the sky becomes gray. By neutralizing luminosity, gray draws attention to light as a source of eventuation and transformation. But, by the same token, gray—or, as in the case of Beckett, the black-grey or the ash grey—is anti dialectical; it "does not come within the realm of clear and distinct ideas."

Some of Wittgenstein's posthumously published remarks on color concur with Badiou's point about the non luminosity of gray. According to Wittgenstein: "Whatever *looks* luminous does not look grey. Everything grey *looks* as though it is being illumined."[11] For Wittgenstein as for Badiou, something that has been grayed out no longer appears as luminous. My claim in this essay is that McCarthy deploys the color gray in *The Road* to register precisely this fact: that the world no longer emits or casts light, that it appears as though it is being illumined—that it is, as a result of the disaster that has befallen it, a "cold illucid world" (123). In one sense, McCarthy pays tribute to Beckett in *The Road* by building a story around the anti dialectical and non luminous aspect of the color gray—by invoking the *noir grise* or the "ash grey" of being. But, in another sense, he distances his novel from Beckett's corpus by trying to isolate a purely human throb in the throat of the apocalypse. McCarthy's fictive purification of being does not result in the pulverized and post human geometry of late Beckett. As I will suggest, it is ultimately the propensity of McCarthy's protagonists to personify in the face of the apocalypse—to humanize the dying biosphere—that separates Beckett gray from McCarthy gray on the color chart of being.

Rather than the sun, which now moves "unseen beyond the murk" (13), what illumines the "cauterised terrain" (13) of *The Road* is the apocalyptic event's shear of light. The ubiquitous grayness of things in this novel has to do with their being overwhelmed almost to the point of extinction by the unexplained disaster. Despite its non appearance in the text, *disaster* is perhaps just the right word to describe the situation—given the fact it comes from the French word for star, *astre*. A now-obsolete meaning of disaster is "An unfavourable aspect of a star or planet; 'an obnoxious planet.'"[12] According to Maurice Blanchot, disaster "means being separated from the star . . . it means the decline which characterizes disorientation when the link with fortune from on high is cut."[13] Here, then, is another way to explain the post-apocalyptic scenario of *The Road*: the bad light from the bad star (the disaster) has displaced the good light from the good star (the sun). Early in the novel, McCarthy captures this crisis of luminosity with a poignant simile: "By day the banished sun circles the earth like a grieving mother with a lamp" (32).

The world as an eye losing its sight, the sun as a grieving mother with a lamp—here we glimpse one of McCarthy's chief rhetorical strategies in *The Road*, which is to rouse our emotions in the post-apocalyptic landscape by personifying those things that have been most affected by the disaster. McCarthy uses the post-apocalyptic scenario in this novel as a kind of thought-experiment through which to isolate the minimal conditions of being human. He thus deploys his poetics of vision not just to register the apocalypse that virtually annihilates the human, but also to relocate the human within the post-apocalypse.

Alex Hunt and Martin M. Jacobsen have observed that the "imagery of light and dark throughout *The Road* recalls Plato's 'Simile of the Sun.'"[14] In the *Republic*, Socrates defines goodness for Plato's brother Glaucon (whose name, incidentally, derives from the Greek word *glaukos*) by proposing an analogy between the visible and the intelligible realms. "As goodness stands in the intelligible realm to intelligence and the things we know," he argues, "so in the visible realm the sun stands to sight and the things we see."[15] Having pointed out that sunlight allows our eyes to perceive objects clearly, Socrates continues to Glaucon:

> 'Well, here's how you can think about the mind as well. When its object is something which is lit up by truth and reality, then it has—and obviously has—intelligent awareness and knowledge. However, when it is permeated with darkness (that is, when its

object is something that is subject to generation and decay), then it has beliefs and is less effective, because its beliefs chop and change, and under these circumstances it comes across as devoid of intelligence. . . . Well, what I'm saying is that it's goodness which gives the things we know their truth and makes it possible for people to have knowledge. It is responsible for knowledge and truth, and you should think of it as being within the intelligible realm, but you shouldn't identify it with knowledge and truth, otherwise you'll be wrong: for all their value, it is even more valuable. In the other realm, it is right to regard light and sight as resembling the sun, but not to identify either of them with the sun.'[16]

In a sense, what Socrates does here is precisely the opposite of what we have seen McCarthy do so far in *The Road*. In contrast to McCarthy, Socrates makes the sun stand outside the realm of the human. His simile depends for its success upon the sun and goodness being ultimately irreducible to the things they condition: light and sight, knowledge and truth.

But what happens to the Platonic conception of the good when a global catastrophe in the form of a long shear of light renders the sun inaccessible to the inhabitants of the earth? What happens, that is, when the source of human perception shifts from being the natural light of the sun to being the sunken gray light of the post-apocalypse?

In *The Road*, what makes the disaster precisely so disastrous is the fact that it bears away with it the very distinction between the sensible and the intelligible. As Hunt and Jacobsen remark, the Platonic conceptualization "is reversed in *The Road*. From the first page, we learn that light and truth are fading. We learn that the world of *The Road* lacks not only valid human perception but even, more disturbingly, the greater truth that makes it possible."[17] With the loss of proper access to the sun comes the loss of the concepts we derive metaphorically from the sun:

The world shrinking down about a raw core of parsible entities. The names of things slowly following those things into oblivion. Colors. The names of birds. Things to eat. Finally the names of things one believed to be true. More fragile than he would have thought. How much was gone already? The sacred idiom shorn of its reality. Drawing down like something trying to preserve heat. In time to wink out forever. (93)

In the *Republic*, Socrates presents our relation to the sun and to goodness as immutable. Since for him the sun and goodness transcend the world, they remain unaffected by whatever happens to it. But McCarthy's text challenges this presumption of ecological stability by positing as its very point of departure the sun's eclipse by the apocalypse. In attributing the grayness of the world to the bad light of the disaster rather than to the good light of the sun, *The Road* renders the truth of the intelligible realm susceptible to the flux of the sensible realm. The disaster substitutes for being the purgatory of the gray in-between. What the novel's post-apocalyptic narrative powerfully imagines is thus something distinctly anti-Platonic: the mortality of concepts and forms: "The names of things slowly following those things into oblivion."

McCarthy radically reorients Platonic thought by graying out the sun and the world in *The Road*. But he certainly doesn't abandon it. This is because the good remains an absolute value in the novel—at least for the central figures of the father and the son. Throughout the story, the son acts as a moral compass for his father, checking the father's survivalist tendencies whenever these result in cruel or amoral behavior toward others. Rather than seeing him (as his father does at one point) as a "Golden chalice, good to house a god" (78), we might just as readily take the boy to be the embodiment of moral goodness. Here, then, is another instance of McCarthy's rhetorical strategy of personification: the personification of the good. In *The Road*, environmental catastrophe has meant that goodness no longer figures as an abstract and transcendent quality that allows for truth and knowledge to take place in the world, but rather has become localized to the point of almost complete relativity.

Goodness is literally embodied in this novel. There are thus the "good guys" and the "bad guys." We see this most clearly in the aftermath of a scene about a third of the way into the novel in which the father is forced to shoot a roaming cannibal in the forehead after this stranger grabs his son. Having cleaned some of the dead man's gore off his child and having tried to sooth both their jangling nerves, the father says to the boy:

You wanted to know what the bad guys looked like. Now you know. It may happen again. My job is to take care of you. I was appointed to do that by God. I will kill anyone who touches you. Do you understand?
Yes.
He sat there cowled in the blanket. After a while he looked up.
Are we still the good guys? he said.
Yes. We're still the good guys.
And we always will be.
Yes. We always will be.
Okay. (80–1)

The poignancy of this scene derives from the absolute fragility of the adverb *always* in it. If to personify something is to render that thing mortal, then the repeated reassurance, "We will always be [the good guys]," is a mortal expression of the persistence of goodness that threatens to expire with the last breath of the father and of the son.

The fragility of the promissory *always* is fully exposed in one of the final and most touching scenes of the novel in which the dying father refuses to take his son with him into the afterlife by shooting the boy with the last bullet in his nickel-plated revolver.

Just take me with you. Please.
I cant.
Please, Papa.
I cant. I cant hold my son dead in my arms. I thought I could but I cant.
You said you wouldnt ever leave me.
I know. I'm sorry. You have my whole heart. You always did. You're the best guy. You always were. If I'm not here you can still talk to me. You can talk to me and I'll talk to you. You'll see.
Will I hear you?
Yes. You will. You have to make it like talk that you imagine. (298)

Here, the father tries to compensate his son for the approaching dissolution of the plural "good guys" into the singular "best guy" by metaphorically offering him his heart and his breath. Until now, the father has watched over the son's every breath with claustrophobic vigilance. When the novel opens his "first instinct . . . is to reach out and touch the boy, to make sure he is still breathing. He is reassured when he feels 'each precious breath' [1], and counts 'each frail breath in the blackness' [13]."[18] Realizing at the end of the novel that he can no longer physically protect his child, the man offers instead the spectral protection of the apostrophe—or the personifying address.

What makes *The Road* such a profound ecological fable is the fact that it presents goodness as being as fragile as any other part of the post-apocalyptic environment. In a 2007 article for *The Guardian* provocatively titled, "Civilisation ends with a shutdown of human concern. Are we there already?", writer and political activist George Monbiot calls *The Road* "the most important environmental book ever written." Monbiot then continues:

> Cormac McCarthy's book *The Road* considers what would happen if the world lost its biosphere, and the only living creatures were humans, hunting for food among the dead wood and soot. Some years before the action begins, the protagonist hears the last birds passing over, "their half-muted crankings miles above where they circled the earth as senselessly as insects trooping the rim of a bowl". McCarthy makes no claim that this is likely to occur, but merely speculates about the consequences.
>
> All pre-existing social codes soon collapse and are replaced with organised butchery, then chaotic, blundering horror. What else are the survivors to do? The only remaining resource is human.[19]

This description of the novel helps us to see why McCarthy opts to personify the things most affected by the disaster—the sun, the world, the good. In a dying world in which the only living creatures are humans (bar, perhaps, a dog that is heard but not seen and "great squid propelling themselves over the floor of the sea in the cold darkness," 234), the pathetic fallacy is perhaps less a fallacy and more a survival strategy. One might say that personification is the last resource of the writer in a world in which the only living thing is human. At the very least, it is a way of registering human concern.

The Road is a bifurcated text. On the one hand, it operates globally and impersonally by rendering the end of the world for us in oftentimes-astonishing, oftentimes-haunting detail. On the other hand, it operates lyrically and locally by addressing the lone—and heroic—attempt by a father and son to survive the "dimming away" of the world by heading south toward a warmer clime. The figurative move that makes sense of this bifurcation, I am arguing, is McCarthy's founding decision to gray out the (Platonic) sun and so render the good in his text solely a matter of the human breath and the human body.

The gray heart

According to anthropologist Michael Taussig in his recent book *What Color Is the Sacred?*, "you cannot separate colour from what it is a colour of."[20] As I've been arguing, gray is a color that marks transition or that preserves the trace of some sort of eventuation. The poetics of gray in *The Road* is a poetics of the post-apocalypse. It is the color of the being of things after the disaster—and this crucially includes the being of the heart. Early in the novel, the father returns, against his son's wishes, to the house where he grew up. When he steps into the doorway of his old bedroom, he starts reminiscing:

> This is where I used to sleep. My cot was against this wall. In the nights in their thousands to dream the dreams of a child's imaginings, worlds rich or fearful such as might offer themselves but never the one to be. He pushed open the closet door half expecting to find his childhood things. Raw cold daylight fell through from the roof. Gray as his heart. (26–7)

Gray signals the return to the present—to the now-empty room with "The wooden lathes of the ceiling exposed" (26). The gray heart is the heart that must take account of the shattering of the world, the perforation of every sacred space and the dimming away of the present after the apocalypse. Apocalypse means revelation. But whatever is revealed to the focalizing consciousness of the father in *The Road*—however rich in detail or color—is just as quickly swallowed up by the all-consuming grayness of the late world: "And the dreams so rich in color. How else would death call you? Waking in the cold dawn it all turned to ash instantly. Like certain ancient frescoes entombed for centuries suddenly exposed to the day" (20).

As Thomas A. Carlson notes, "*The Road* engages us in a meditation—both literary and religious—on the essential interplay of world and heart."[21] What the novel suggests to us through the central example of the relationship between the father and son is that heart and world are not reducible to one another—even in a worst-case or post-apocalyptic scenario. Holding the gray heart apart from the gray world in *The Road* is its power to personify—or to project a kind of bare life onto an apparently lifeless exterior. This, one might say, is the heart's handiness in a time of absolute physical crisis. Personification thus finally figures in McCarthy's novel as an existential survival strategy. It is what allows the father and son to take the next step of their journey, as they project themselves to be "carrying the fire" or embodying goodness in an otherwise illucid world.

Significantly, personification is also a power that the boy's mother is shown to lack in the analeptic dialogue in which she justifies her decision to suicide.

> We're survivors he told her across the flame of the lamp.
> Survivors? she said.
> Yes.
> What in God's name are you talking about? We're not survivors. We're the walking dead in a horror film. (57)

The mother's heart fails because it fails to breathe life into the grayed-out things of the post-apocalypse. For her, death has arrived with the long shear of light that stopped all the clocks at 1:17—and any survivors are merely walking dead.

> We used to talk about death, she said. We dont any more. Why is that?
> I dont know.
> It's because it's here. There's nothing left to talk about. (58)

The mother thus approaches the graying out of the world without hope or heart.

> You talk about taking a stand but there is no stand to take. My heart was ripped out of me the night he was born so dont ask

for sorrow now. There is none. Maybe you'll be good at this. I doubt it, but who knows. The one thing I can tell you is that you wont survive for yourself. I know because I would never have come this far. A person who had no one would be well advised to cobble together some passable ghost. Breathe it into being and coax it along with words of love. Offer it each phantom crumb and shield it from harm with your body. As for me my only hope is for eternal nothingness and I hope it with all my heart. (59)

Having by her own admission lost the power to preserve her heart from the bad light of the disaster, the mother finally succumbs to it. It is significant, then, that she commits suicide with a flake of obsidian, a naturally occurring volcanic glass that, depending on how it is cut, appears jet black or glistening gray.

"Perhaps in the world's destruction it would be possible at last to see how it was made. Oceans, mountains. The ponderous counterspectacle of things ceasing to be" (293). So muses the narrative voice late in the novel. What the "ponderous counterspectacle of things ceasing to be" in *The Road* also shows us is how the heart is made. The mother is right to tell the father he won't survive the post-apocalypse for himself. As Carlson writes: "The heart, in whose light alone any possibility of world or life at all appear for him, belongs not to him, alone, but to his being-with the fragile and threatened child who himself never knew the world—having been born only after the unnamed catastrophe, and thereby opening, or incarnating, the question of what birth and its promise could mean in the ostensible absence of any time for expectation or memory."[22] The mother concludes the same thing as the father after the disaster: that the heart avoids becoming mortified by breathing life into the other. The difference—and the cause of her despair—is that she now sees this as a purely hypothetical, fantastical, or imaginary act: the stuff of literature rather than of life. The son buffers the father against the disaster by embodying the personifying heart. But as if to indicate the real tenuousness of this situation, there are moments in the novel when the boy starts to resemble what his mother calls a "passable ghost": "The boy's candlecoloured skin was all but translucent" (137); "Ghostly pale and shivering. The boy so thin it stopped his heart" (39).

The gray fire

In a 2007 book review for *The New Republic*, "Getting to the End," James Wood faults *The Road* for "being personal at the moment when it should be theological." According to Wood:

> to compare McCarthy to Beckett, as some reviewers have done,[23] is to flatter McCarthy. His reticence and his minimalism work superbly at evocation, but they exhaust themselves when philosophy presses down. The style that is so good at the glancing, the lyrical, the half-expressed struggles to deal adequately with the metaphysical questions that apocalypse raises. Beyond tiny hints, we have no idea what the father and son believe about God's survival, so there is no dramatized rendition, no aesthetically responsible account, of such a question.[24]

Contra Wood, I've been arguing in this essay that McCarthy's reticence and minimalism do not exhaust themselves when philosophy presses down upon them. What Wood misses in his review of *The Road* is the significance of McCarthy's poetics of gray, which profoundly reorients Plato's "Simile of the Sun" by rendering goodness a concept whose truth-value must be measured against the event-horizon of ecological catastrophe. In the gray light of the disaster, goodness becomes, like the brook trout of the novel's final paragraph, "a thing which could not be put back. Not be made right again" (307).

The question in *The Road* is less what the father and son believe about God's survival and more how they use God to survive. Jay Ellis aptly describes the father as "*Homo techne*": "He must do, in order to survive and secure the survival of his son. . . . He must always act with utilitarian efficiency. This comes out in the many Hemingwayesque passages of fixing things, using tools."[25] The journeying pair comes to scrutinize everything in this novel in terms of its potential handiness—and God and the good perhaps prove no exception to this rule of thumb. McCarthy makes the personal and the theological intersect in *The Road* by developing a theology of the personifying heart. As we see in the novel's penultimate paragraph, this theology of the personifying heart gently defaces the terms and conditions of traditional Christianity by being a metaphysical survival strategy:

> The woman when she saw him put her arms around him and held him. Oh, she said, I am so glad to see you. She would talk

to him sometimes about God. He tried to talk to God but the best thing was to talk to his father and he did talk to him and he didnt forget. The woman said that was all right. She said that the breath of God was his breath yet though it pass from man to man through all of time. (306)

For Wood: "the placement of what looks like a paragraph of religious consolation at the end of such a novel is striking, and it throws the novel off balance, precisely because theology has not seemed exactly central to the novel's inquiry."[26] Rather than throwing the novel off balance, I find this paragraph entirely consistent with its overarching rhetorical strategy of personifying the grayed out things of the post-apocalypse. Where McCarthy differs from a writer such as Beckett is in allowing his characters not only to articulate but also to make clear existential choices. As we have already seen, the mother chooses despair over hope, death over life—and, here, the son prefers to keep talking to his dead father rather than to God. As Shelly L. Rambo notes: "In the aftermath of the collapse of the world [in *The Road*], there is no end in sight, no destination, and no promise of life ahead. But in the face of these impossibilities, the impulse to impose redemption is replaced, instead, by an imperative to witness to what remains."[27] The boy feels he can continue on after the disaster and after the loss of his father only by personifying God and the good. He chooses to commemorate the mortal breath of the father rather than the immortal breath of God. In so doing, he acknowledges the continuing fragility of both the world and the heart.

Having begun this essay with one of Wittgenstein's reflections on color, it is perhaps appropriate for me to end with another. In *Remarks on Colour*, Wittgenstein proposes the following inductive puzzle: "I am told that a substance burns with a grey flame. I don't know the colours of the flames of all substances; so why shouldn't that be possible?"[28] Where better to imagine the possibility of a gray flame than in a work of post-apocalyptic literature in which everything appears grayed out due to some unexplained catastrophe? The father and son see themselves as "carrying the fire" in *The Road*. This is a "kind of familial shorthand . . . a version of being the 'good guys'" (Wood). "Are you carrying the fire?" (303), asks the boy of the man with the "gray and yellow ski parka" (301) who finds him three—symbolic?—days after his father dies. Is it possible that this metaphysical fire—this fragile token of goodness in a world dichotomized by apocalypse—burns with a gray flame? Is the final thing that McCarthy personifies for us in *The Road* the color gray?

"If one of the most 'sacred' aims that man can set for himself is to acquire as exact and intense an understanding of himself as possible," writes Michel Leiris in his 1938 essay "The Sacred in Everyday Life," "it seems desirable that each one, scrutinizing his memories with the greatest possible honesty, examine whether he can discover there some sign permitting him to discern the *color* for him of the very notion of the sacred."[29] In this essay, Leiris goes through a number of everyday objects that awaken in him "that mixture of fear and attachment, that ambiguous attitude caused by the approach of something simultaneously attractive and dangerous, prestigious and outcast—that combination of respect, desire, and terror that we take as a psychological sign of the sacred"[30]: his father's flat-brimmed top hat, a small-barreled, nickel-plated Smith and Wesson and money box, a salamander stove the family owned, his parent's bedroom, the bathroom. What awakens the feeling of the sacred in *The Road*, I would suggest, is not any object in particular but rather the gray post-apocalyptic light in which every object in the novel is bathed. For McCarthy, it is the dimming away of the object—its growing faint from grayness—that enables us, at last, to see how it was made.

Notes

1   Ludwig Wittgenstein, *Culture and Value*, eds. G. H. von Wright and H. Nyman, trans. Peter Winch, revised Edition of the Text by Alois Pichler (Oxford: Basil Blackwell, 1998), 76.

2   Richard Gray, "Open Doors, Closed Minds: American Prose Writing at a Time of Crisis," *American Literary History* 21.1 (2009): 137.

3   Samuel Beckett, *Endgame* (London: Faber and Faber, 1963), 11.

4   Beckett, *Endgame*, 25.

5   Beckett, *Endgame*, 26.

6   Hugh Kenner, *Samuel Beckett: A Critical Study* (Berkeley: University of California Press, 1973), 155.

7   Andrew Gibson, *Beckett and Badiou: the Pathos of Intermittency* (New York: Oxford University Press, 2006), 237.

8   Alain Badiou, *Conditions*, trans. Steven Corcoran (London and New York: Continuum, 2008), 255. I am grateful to Julian Murphet for directing me toward Alain Badiou's work on Beckett.

9   Quoted in Badiou, *Conditions*, 255–6.

10 Badiou, *Conditions*, 256.

11 Wittgenstein, *Remarks on Colour*, ed. G. E. M. Anscombe, trans. Linda L. McAlister and Margarete Schättle (Oxford: Basil Blackwell, 1978), 47e, original emphasis.

12 "Disaster, *n.*" *The Oxford English Dictionary*. 2nd ed. 1989.

13 Maurice Blanchot, *The Writing of the Disaster*, trans. Ann Smock (Lincoln and London: University of Nebraska Press, 1995), 2.

14 Alex Hunt and Martin M. Jacobsen, "Cormac McCarthy's *The Road* and Plato's 'Simile of the Sun,'" *Explicator* 66.3 (2008): 156.

15 Plato, *Republic*, trans. Robin Waterfield (London: The Folio Society, 2003), 257.

16 Plato, *Republic*, 257–8.

17 Hunt and Jacobsen, "Cormac McCarthy's *The Road*," 156.

18 Susan J. Tyburski, "'The Lingering Scent of Divinity' in *The Sunset Limited* and *The Road*," *The Cormac McCarthy Journal* 6 (2008): 125.

19 George Monbiot, "Civilisation ends with a shutdown of human concern. Are we there already?" *The Guardian* 30 Oct. 2007. Web. 1 March 2010.

20 Michael Taussig, *What Color Is the Sacred?* (Chicago and London: The University of Chicago Press, 2009), 250.

21 Thomas A. Carlson, "With the World at Heart: Reading Cormac McCarthy's *The Road* with Augustine and Heidegger," *Religion and Literature* 39.3 (2007): 5.

22 Carlson, "With the World at Heart," 55.

23 Richard Gray finds McCarthy's characters as existentially resilient as those of Beckett. According to Gray, "*The Road* surely echoes, in its structure and feeling if not literally, Samuel Beckett's attempt to name *The Unnameable* (1958): 'I don't know, I'll never know, in the silence you don't know, you must go on, I can't go on, I'll go on'" (139).

24 James Wood, "Getting to the End," review of *The Road*, by Cormac McCarthy, *The New Republic* 21 May 2007. Web. 3 March 2010.

25 Jay Ellis, "Another Sense of Ending: The Keynote Address to the Knoxville Conference," *The Cormac McCarthy Journal* 6 (2008): 22–38. 30.

26 Wood, "Getting to the End."

27 Shelly L. Rambo, "Beyond Redemption: Reading Cormac McCarthy's *The Road* After the End of the World," *Studies in Literary Imagination* 41.2 (2008): 115.

28 Wittgenstein, *Remarks on Colour*, 7.

29 Michel Leiris, "The Sacred in Everyday Life," in *The College of Sociology*, ed. D. Hollier, trans. Betsy Wing (Minneapolis: University of Minnesota Press, 1988), 31. This passage inspired Taussig to title his book *What Color Is the Sacred?* Leiris in fact got the idea of the color of the sacred from Colette Poignot, the companion of Georges Bataille who died of tuberculosis in 1938. "What color does the very sacred have for me?" (quoted in Hollier 100), writes Poignot in a posthumous collection of notes, published by Leiris and Bataille under the title *Le Sacré*.

30 Leiris, "The Sacred in Everyday Life," 24.

3

McCarthy's rhythm

SEAN PRYOR

"When he woke in the woods in the dark and the cold of the night he'd reach out" (1)—five anapests and a bacchius? Only if we indulge preposterously in scanning contemporary American prose with classical feet. The light of ancient Greece is not so very far from this post-apocalyptic waking in the dark, the opening phrase of Cormac McCarthy's *The Road*, for we soon learn that the man has woken from a dream that twists Plato's allegory of the cave.[1] But that hardly seems sufficient warrant, and before we come even to argue for the justice of classical scansion, there is the problem that this is prose. Does it matter that a novel's first fifteen syllables slip into lilting triplets and that the next three do not? McCarthy could so easily have continued that lilt by expanding his contraction—"in the dark and the cold of the night he would reach out to touch"—but instead that regular pulse is interrupted. Or perhaps the syllables syncopate over a beat. An attentive or inventive listener might decide the interruption marks the man's solicitude, the shift to emphatic contiguous stresses signaling the shift from involuntary wakening to deliberate action: "reach out." When that new rhythm sounds a second time, it marks the object of concern, the man's son, before the sentence then resumes its triple lilt: "the child sleeping beside him."[2]

The meaning of McCarthy's rhythm is complicated by his grammar, for the habitual aspect of the first sentence describes not a single action but repeated actions. Whenever the man woke in the night, he reached out for the boy. The shape of that sentence might be said to mime a recurrent experience, arcing from sleep, through anxiety, to a wary but familiar waking. The rhythm of a single sentence would then follow the rhythm of a single event, but also participate in a larger rhythm of events. There is a comparable effect two sentences later, when a different rhythm mimes inhalation and exhalation: "His hand rose and fell softly with each precious breath" (1). Those twinned stresses—*hand rose, fell soft-, each pre-* —seem neatly to match the contraction and relaxation of a diaphragm. With its ambiguous aspect, the sentence combines the breaths the boy takes night after night and the breaths he takes one cold dark night. It's that specific night which grounds the next sentence, as McCarthy's narrative proper begins: "He pushed away the plastic tarpaulin and raised himself in the stinking robes and blankets" (1). But the twinned stresses also align the boy's breathing with McCarthy's writing. For a time, the boy's chest, the man's hand, and the novel's words share a rhythm, a biological order which supports and encompasses the events that follow.

At this point, a skeptical reader might judge that such thoughts are much too far-fetched, and settle down for a gripping page turner, an epochal meditation on ecological collapse, or a brilliant genre exercise in adventure and horror.[3] This attention to rhythm may not have been intended when Oprah's Book Club suggested readers ask how *The Road* is more like poetry than prose.[4] Such rhythms may not have been what John Hillcoat, director of the 2009 film of the novel, meant when he called McCarthy's writing "a form of poetry," nor even what William Kennedy meant in praising McCarthy's "rhythmic poetry."[5] In the press and in the blogosphere, readers extolled the novel's poetry and lyricism.[6] Presuming an older hierarchy of literary genres, those labels sometimes seem nothing more than loose ways to express approval. The situation is somewhat ironic, since McCarthy's prose has little in common with contemporary poetry, however traditional or avant-garde.

But even a skeptical reader might pause when, for the third time in only its first paragraph, *The Road* offers yet another striking rhythm. In the dream from which the man has woken, we read, he and the boy wander in a cave that drips with water: "Tolling in the silence the minutes of the earth and the hours and the days of it and the years without cease" (1). Here McCarthy overlays syllabic with syntactic rhythms. Pairs of strong stresses portion out those first two phrases, each of which turns on a prepositional qualification: "Tolling in the silence," "the minutes of the earth." A triple rhythm shapes the next pair of stresses, aligned by a common prepositional tag: "and the hours and the days of it." And then that polysyndeton compels yet another pair in triplets: "and the years without cease." This complex rhythm structures the sentence's steady expansion from single drops, through minutes, hours, days, and years, to eternity. If the earlier sentence linked McCarthy's writing to biology, this sentence links it to the order of the solar system.

To do this, McCarthy reaches for that archaic noun *cease*, fossilized in the still occasionally current phrase "without cease." Readers often remark on McCarthy's loving assemblage of obsolete and obscure words. *The Road* is very clearly concerned with the way an apocalypse might change language and its attention to dead and dying words anticipates that change. The archaism also signals vast eons. Like the parataxis, it suggests a biblical scope: "While the earth remaineth, seedtime and harvest, and cold and heat, and summer and winter, and day and night shall not cease" (Genesis 8.22). But the archaic noun and the biblical echo are also ironic; the brief life cycles of a word and a tradition are offset by the expanse of inhuman time. McCarthy's diction and syntax are allusive, and that depends on human history, but there is also a mimetic logic which indicates an order beyond that history. The rhythm of words suggests the movement of the cosmos. But how can a novel link its language to the rhythms of a single narrative, to the biological rhythms that sustain human life, and to the celestial rhythms of slowly turning planets? How can it do that *and* so ostentatiously lament the transformation of language occasioned by a single cataclysm? For though that cataclysm dictates McCarthy's narrative, though it has ended the migratory cycles of birds (54–5), and thought it might yet snuff out human life, it leaves the constant cosmos unaffected. If there were still a crow to fly above the thick ashen clouds, the man explains, it would find the sun going about its usual business (168).

To begin to think through these problems, we should note that, if scanning prose or interpreting its rhythms is troubling, it may be because we associate significant rhythm with poetry. When Wordsworth turns his consonants and vowels in time to earth's diurnal course, the artifice can seem natural to the genre, a genre which may not be as old as the earth but which has witnessed the earth's turning for some time. If the novel represents an hour in literary history, our records of poetry stretch perhaps from dawn to midday. Neither is as constant as the music of the spheres, but poetry is a comparatively archaic form and in McCarthy's other novels he puts this difference to work. *Blood Meridian* begins with a child whose drunk father "quotes from poets whose names are now lost."[7] The introductory portrait of that child ends with an ironic reference to Wordsworth that separates the time of poetry from the time of this novel, a time when childhood wonderment could survive into adulthood from a time when that innocence is always already lost: "He can neither read nor write and in him broods already a taste for mindless violence. All history present in that visage, the child the father of the man." McCarthy's allusions to and adaptations of past poets, from Dante and Milton to Blake and Eliot, help to set hellish scenes and paint waste landscapes, but they also suggest that poetic tradition's collapse. The religious, moral, and literary systems of past poets are unable to account for the new world of this novel, and might even now prove oppressive. It's no accident that the judge reads the Greek poets and declaims in "the old epic mode."[8]

McCarthy's own "poetry" is another matter. Reading *The Road*, James Wood remains cautious:

> Hard detail and a fine eye is combined with exquisite, gnarled, slightly antique (and even slightly clumsy or heavy) lyricism. It ought not to work, and sometimes it does not. But many of its effects are beautiful — and not only beautiful, but powerfully efficient as poetry.[9]

For Wood, McCarthy's lyricism is tied up with that lexical archaeology; for others, it might involve only the timbre of odd words: *balefires* (15), *salitter* (279), *wimpled* (307). But earlier in the review, Wood describes McCarthy's distinctive syntax, with its probing repetitions and plodding simplicity, as a "dumbly questing, glacially heuristic approach [that] matches its subject, a world in which nothing is left standing." That *matching* seems, more than anything else, to motivate the label "poetry" and make the poetry efficient. It's as if Pope's old maxim on sound and sense were given new urgency by the apocalypse. McCarthy's sentences match the movements of the man and boy, just as his stresses echo the boy's breathing or as alliteration sounds the bodily rhythms of the monster in the man's dream: "Its bowels, its beating heart. The brain that pulsed in a dull glass bell" (2). Applying the same logic to the larger structures of the narrative, Richard Gray comments that McCarthy's "continuous series of discrete paragraphs undivided into chapters or sections, clearly repeats the rhythm of the journey."[10]

But what would make poetry in prose clumsy, heavy, or only beautiful? The lexical display, probably, but also the carefully sonorous rhythms, and maybe that brazen mimesis, too.[11] Our justification would probably be that each of these were in some way unnecessary or unnatural. What purpose, other than a bid for attention, is served by the thick rhyme and assonance in a phrase like "stared into the light with eyes dead white and sightless as the eggs of spiders" (2)? (Or do those preposterous repetitions somehow match the enormity of that dream-monster?)[12] One might insist that poets and novelists stick to their proper genres. Hazlitt complained that when poets trespass in prose their beloved ornaments become merely "pleasing excrescences." A poet writing in prose too often adorns his "patch-work" with "tinsel finery at random, in despair, without propriety, and without effect."[13] There is nothing efficient about most poets' prose, he argues, for the usual subjects of prose demand a different style. Still, Hazlitt believes that style and subject should at some level match in both good prose and good verse. Wood and Gray seem sure that, at least at their best, McCarthy's rhythms do suit his post-apocalyptic world, though the kind of correspondence could be said to infringe on poetry's estate. The trouble would not be that McCarthy's finery has no effect, but that its effects are not proper to prose. Most thinking about prose rhythm has indeed focused on abstract proprieties rather than mimesis: the balance of a period, the force of a cadence, the euphony of variety.[14] So rhythm in prose might be clumsy, heavy, or merely beautiful when, with all the art it can muster, it aims at something else.

Quintilian warns that sounding a complete line of verse in prose is especially loathsome ("foedissimum"), and that even part of a line is likely to be ugly ("deforme").[15] His term *deformis*, meaning deformed or misshapen, is acute. The sounding of poetry in prose might ordinarily be considered less a lack of form than an excess, an intrusion of artificial meter into the natural sequences of prose. But Quintilian suggests that prose, or good prose, has its distinct and proper rhythm, and we may ask, too, whether prose rhythm has its distinct and proper function. Aristotle pursues this problem at length:

> The form of the language should be neither metrical nor unrhythmical. The former is unpersuasive (for it seems to have been consciously shaped) and at the same time also diverts attention; for it causes [the listener] to pay attention to when the same foot will come again . . . But what is unrhythmical is unlimited, and there should be a limit, but not by use of meter; for the unlimited is unpleasant and unknowable. And all things are limited by number. In the case of the form of language, number is rhythm, of which the meters are segments. Thus, speech should have rhythm but not meter; for the latter will be a poem. The rhythm should not be exact. This will be achieved if it is [regular] only up to a point.[16]

McCarthy's rhythms could certainly be accused of distracting the reader's attention, and after that first paragraph, it can be difficult not to keep an ear out for unusually regular or neatly mimetic patterns. One irony is that these deliberate, "artificial" rhythms frequently match natural phenomena. But the logic of that matching is one of cosmic correspondence: heartbeats, breaths, waking and sleeping, days and nights, safety and danger, food and hunger, travel and rest, action and thought, question and answer, speech and silence, life and death—all conform to rhythms sounded by McCarthy's language. Life like language in *The Road* is limited by number. There is an order to a cosmos.

This is not what Quintilian envisages when he cautions against the inclusion of familiar poetic meters. For Quintilian, a large part of the problem would be that the prose rhythm involves a distracting or irrelevant allusion, as if McCarthy's opening triplets evoked Byron's gallop: "The Assyrian came down like the wolf on the fold, And his cohorts were gleaming in purple and gold."[17] Critics do sometimes trace allusions in this way, if not to poems then to genres and traditions. Hugh Kenner once scanned the first words of *Ulysses* as a heroic hexameter,[18] and *The Road* occasionally engages in this kind of play. At an odd moment the man carves for the boy a makeshift flute from a piece of roadside cane, and "after a while the man could hear him playing. A formless music for the age to come" (81).[19] Two neat lines of blank verse sound the formed music of an age now lost, offering like McCarthy's archaic lexicon a sign of civilization's fall.

This effect is unusual, and yet *The Road* does not quite fit Aristotle's account of prose rhythm either, for Aristotle attributes specific tones, moods, or effects to particular rhythms: dactyls are dignified; iambs evoke common speech; trochees run or trip.[20] One might call those opening triplets relatively relaxed, but it's especially tempting to read McCarthy's syntactic rhythms this way:

> He pulled the blue plastic tarp off of him and folded it and carried it out to the grocery cart and packed it and came back with their plates and some cornmeal cakes in a plastic bag and a plastic bottle of soup. (3)

Polysyndeton can seem to convey a flat, mechanical routine, moving indifferently through actions and objects. Or, as before, it can convey the inexorable passing of time. But it can just as readily be swift and exciting:

> He shoved the pistol in his belt and slung the knapsack over his shoulder and picked up the boy and turned him around and lifted him over his head and set him on his shoulders and set off up the old roadway at a dead run[.] (69)

Neither triple rhythms nor polysyndeton has, in *The Road*, a fixed signification.

This is important because it helps to explain why McCarthy's attention to rhythm is distinct from, and often in conflict with, his attention to names. At one point, the man thinks of the post-apocalyptic transformation of language as the death of names: "The names of things slowly following those things into oblivion" (93). *Blue* no longer refers to a color, or to the sky, or to the sea. *Beauty* no longer means. Were McCarthy's rhythms merely allusive or inherently meaningful they too might be subject to this death. But for McCarthy, rhythms do not die with names. Though rhythm is perceptual, requiring a subject to relate or identify phenomena, it is not peculiar to language, to semiotic systems, or to human history. The sky and the sea have their own rhythms, with which the rhythms of prose may coincide. A rhythm need not be the name of a thing, nor need it mean anything on its own. So we need to listen to rhythms, as well as to names, in order to understand how *The Road* positions itself in relation to that apocalypse.

We need also to consider Aristotle's distinction between the meaning of a rhythm and the meaning of rhythm. A trochee may trip, but number is a bulwark against chaos. This gives it particular value in *The Road*, a novel which routinely invokes the dark, the "void" (10), the "blackness without depth or dimension" (70), the land "shadowless and without feature" (189), the days "uncounted and uncalendered" (292)—a world seemingly without difference or limitation, in space and time. After all, an apocalypse ought properly to end rhythm as we know it, an unnameable and unrepeatable event that forever changes the condition of events, or even an event that ends events altogether, heralding eternity or oblivion.

McCarthy's apocalyptic event has passed before *The Road* begins, but other unnameable events echo that singularity, seeming to confirm that change in the way things happen:

> He got up and walked out to the road. The black shape of it running from dark to dark. Then a distant low rumble. Not thunder. You could feel it under your feet. A sound without cognate and so without description. Something imponderable shifting out there in the dark. The earth itself contracting with the cold. It did not come again. What time of year? What age the child? (279)

On the one hand, this passage provides another anxious meditation on the transformation of language; on the other, McCarthy's ever so resonant rhythms assimilate the indescribable. The man or the narrator is careful, first, to refuse the association of the names *rumble* and *thunder*. No hackneyed literary idiom can describe this post-apocalyptic phenomenon.[21] But the sounds of that refusal aptly rumble and echo: *running*, *rumble*, *thunder*, *under*, and then, at a distance, *imponderable*. The sequence of sentences seems, in its rhythmic contraction, to echo the rumble's dissipation:

> Something imponderable shifting out there in the dark.
> The earth itself contracting with the cold.
> It did not come again.
> What time of year?
> What age the child?

—what we might call a probing pentameter in triplets and quadruplets, a terse iambic pentameter, a severe trimeter, and two bewildered dimeters. If the effect seems ugly, deformed, or artificial, it's partly because McCarthy has to do such violence to his syntax in order to achieve it. (Why not "What time of year was it"? Why not "How old was the child"?)

But more plausible than any obvious sonic correspondence is a mimesis of the rhythms of thought. The man or the narrator first attempts to describe the indescribable with that vague "Something" and the privative "imponderable." He moves then to a more specific reformulation, linked to the first effort by another participle but newly speculating about a cause. The next sentence reflects on the sound's singularity and its temporality, as if having paused to listen in the silence for recurrences, before two questions are then put to that silence, questions prompted by the sound's relation to planetary movement and human time. This local rhythm of thought takes its place, in turn, in larger rhythms of narration. The paragraph shifts from an omniscient account of the man rising and approaching the road, to the freer focalization of what seem to be his thoughts. (Is it the prominence given to the man's subjectivity that makes the novel "lyrical"?) *The Road* routinely follows an action or actions with a sequence of observations and speculations in just this way; full sentences give way to verbless phrases. The pattern recurs immediately:

> What age the child? He walked out into the road and stood. The silence. The salitter drying from the earth. The mudstained shapes of flooded cities burned to the waterline. At a crossroads a ground set with dolmen stones where the spoken bones or oracles lay moldering. No sound but the wind. What will you say? (279)

Finally, the rhythm of thought is managed by the periodic contraction and expansion of McCarthy's sentences.[22] It's especially clear in this passage because both moments of contraction also indicate that silence and prompt questions. Earlier on the same page, the man and boy having set out along the road, another series of observations pauses on that same simple phrase, "The silence." Like the near verbatim repetition of walking out (in)to the road, this only highlights the presence of recurrent patterns—of phoneme, stress, diction, syntax, and paragraph. At a larger scale again, this episode of cautious approach, rumble, and reflection forms a kind of narrative diastole, a relaxation after a tense encounter, the systole in which the man and the boy, having had their possessions stolen, catch the thief and leave him naked and destitute in the road. Walking out to or into the road forms a narrative ostinato, followed invariably by fleeing the road for safety or leaving it in search of food.

What does it mean to give life after the apocalypse rhythm in this way, to give it shape and order? If there is a difference between names and rhythms, perhaps *The Road* sounds the miserable rhythms of this new world, even when using the names of the old. That might constitute the poetry's efficient beauty or give substance to the label "lyrical," as if McCarthy had formed a music to match the age to come. Post-apocalyptic rhythms replace the novel's traditional arc of crisis and resolution with the cycle of life and death. Most miserable might be the new world's indifference to the singularity of death, for McCarthy's verbal repetitions blur individuals even at that most private moment: "He slept close to his father that night and held him but when he woke in the morning his father was cold and stiff" (300). The man's death finishes the novel, but the pronouns' anonymity means the boy takes up well established rhythms without interruption: "when he woke in the morning."[23] Soon after, just as his father had, "he walked out to the road and he looked down the road" (301). Here rhythm signals the cruel indifference of biological succession, made ironic by the threat of humanity's extinction.

Yet that succession is hardly peculiar to this waste world. Moreover, this is precisely what the man has told the boy to do:

> You need to go on, he said. I cant go with you. You need to keep going. You dont know what might be down the road. We were always lucky. You'll be lucky again. You'll see. Just go. It's all right. I cant.
> It's all right. This has been a long time coming. Now it's here. Keep going south. Do everything the way we did it. (297)

The boy learns his lesson well. Having walked out to the road, he is lucky: another man arrives, ready to take him in and give him a family. We're not told whether, after the novel, the boy and his adoptive family keep going south, but we do know that their life together is ordered by repetitions: "She would talk to him sometimes about God. He tried to talk to God but the best thing was to talk to his father and he did talk to him and he didnt forget" (306). As *The Road* withdraws from its episodic narrative, that return to the habitual aspect with which it began allows the rhythms of their talk to continue. The boy's ongoing conversations with his father represent another lesson well learnt. They give order to this future beyond the novel, an order that the novel has already established in the man's and the boy's patterned dialogues and silences. This is just as his father counseled: "If I'm not here you can still talk to me. You can talk to me and I'll talk to you. . . . You have to make it like talk that you imagine. And you'll hear me. You have to practice" (298–9). And practice he does, even before the man has died: "He closed his eyes and talked to him and he kept his eyes closed and listened. Then he tried again" (299).

This post-apocalyptic adaptation of the ritual of prayer plays neatly into the novel's turn to religion, but it complicates the meaning of McCarthy's rhythm. A fugitive trudge across a dead planet may be a limited life, but dialogue and prayer give that life value. There are rhythms that must be suffered, and others that must be cultivated. The problem of the value of rhythm in prose is related to the problem of its value in life. Aristotle advocates rhythmic prose because without rhythm, without limitation by number, prose would be unlimited, and that which is unlimited is unpleasant and unknowable. The boy may not pipe Mozart, but he too feels the value of number when, each night, he sits by the fire with their map, tracing their journey: "He had the names of towns and rivers by heart and he measured their progress daily" (229). He turns movement across undifferentiated space and through undifferentiated time into a rhythm. So, too, in the night the man holds the boy to him and "count[s] each frail breath" (13). So is it then that *The Road* embraces the apocalypse in familiar and comforting orders? Its religious, biological, and celestial rhythms stretch before and after the brief interval of its narrative, and in conspicuously beautiful harmonies, its verbal rhythms match even the most miserable experiences. It is as if McCarthy's rhythm redeems the wasteland.

The trouble is that, for all the comfort of number, McCarthy's post-apocalyptic world is not simply a chaos. This cosmos is miserably rhythmic:

He walked out in the gray light and stood and he saw for a
brief moment the absolute truth of the world. The cold relentless
circling of the intestate earth. Darkness implacable. The blind
dogs of the sun in their running. The crushing black vacuum of
the universe. And somewhere two hunted animals trembling like
ground-foxes in their cover. Borrowed time and borrowed world
and borrowed eyes with which to sorrow it. (138)

Like clockwork, McCarthy's vowels fall into place to tick the
turning earth: -lent-, circ-, -test-, earth.[24] As before, this mimesis is
bought at the cost of ironic archaism: a transitive sorrow to rhyme
with borrow, rather than a more ordinary mourn or lament. And
the thought of these monotonous, inhuman, celestial rhythms is
oppressive. They throw in relief the all too vulnerable biological
and dialogic rhythms cherished by the man and the boy. The
apocalypse seems then to have altered the meaning of the order
of the cosmos, or rather to have exposed its meaning. It's curious
how ahistoric that formulation is: the absolute truth of the world.
The terms apocalypse and revelation never appear in The Road,
but the one instance of reveal suggests just this unchanging truth:
"The frailty of everything revealed at last" (28). There is nothing
specifically post-apocalyptic about that truth, and there is nothing
newly frail about life.[25]

Indeed, the final paragraph of the novel, standing apart from
the narrative, makes it clear that the earth has only pursued its
inevitable fate. What looks like a lament for a genuine apocalypse is
really a recognition that the fires of the wasteland were lit long ago.
The brook trout and their flowing stream may have disappeared,
but that disappearance is part of the world's own flow: "On their
backs were vermiculate patterns that were maps of the world in
its becoming. Maps and mazes. Of a thing which could not be put
back. Not be made right again" (307). The event which cannot be
canceled or corrected is not that shear of light (54) but the world
itself, its creation. According to some more fundamental fall, the
world was always already wrong.[26] And if rhythm is the form of
flow (ῥυθμός, from ῥεῖν, to flow), then McCarthy concludes that
nothing is exempt from the rhythm of the cosmos.

This neatly inverts Aristotle's sense of number as the ground of
pleasure. It stands in even more stark contradiction to Plato, for
whom the order of the cosmos is both beautiful and good. In The

Republic, rhythm has a moral dimension that makes it central to pedagogy:

> education in music is most sovereign, because more than anything
> else rhythm and harmony find their way to the inmost soul and
> take strongest hold upon it, bringing with them and imparting
> grace . . . And further, because omissions and the failure of
> beauty in things badly made or grown would be most quickly
> perceived by one who was properly educated in music, and so,
> feeling distaste rightly, he would praise beautiful things and take
> delight in them and receive them into his soul to foster its growth
> and become himself beautiful and good.[27]

It's telling, then, that the relationship between McCarthy's man and boy is characterized by a kind of pedagogic impasse. The man can carve his son a flute, but seems unable or unwilling to teach him how to play it. The man can show him how to make a lamp from a bottle and a rag (143), but the boy no longer takes lessons in writing (262) and, most importantly, he refuses to adopt the man's morality. As has often been noted, the boy meets the man's hard, pragmatic individualism with charity and fellow-feeling. Suggestively, that opening dream depicts not pedagogy but andragogy: "In the dream from which he'd wakened he had wandered in a cave where the child led him by the hand" (1). The boy's refusal to be taught certainly makes him sympathetic, since the man's morality is sometimes quite objectionable. As McCarthy explained in an interview, virtue or nobility in *The Road* is natural, innate: "I don't think goodness is something that you learn."[28]

The exception is that final lesson, the lesson of prayer. Throughout their journey the boy has periodically refused or been reluctant to talk, at times in response to some new horror but often in response to a choice the man has made about whether to help others (53, 71, 80, 98, 185, 279, 286, 288–9). Yet at the end talking to his dead father proves to be "the best thing," a phrase that directly echoes the man's parting benediction: "You're the best guy. You always were" (298). Playing on that ambiguous adjective, the novel gives to conversation or prayer a moral value, in addition to its function as pleasure or comfort. It isn't necessarily that the boy finally inherits the man's morality, but that he allows their differences to continue. The boy comes to learn not only that a waste world can be redeemed by beautiful rhythms, but that it should be. Yet the rhythms of that world have their moral value too. The earth's relentless circling may be miserable to think of, a force to which we must passively submit, but it is also immoral: "Not be made *right* again."

Where does that leave McCarthy and his novel? There are two problems posed by *The Road*: what to do? and what to write? The man and the boy confront a series of moral dilemmas, but to the extent that goodness is not something you can learn, and that moral character is not something you can control, their choices are predetermined. The boy's graceful soul may rightly discern the good and the bad, but no education has achieved this. The lesson of prayer is important, then, as an exception to that rule. It resolves the pedagogic impasse and grounds morality. It is a kind of resistance, a deliberate effort opposed to the state of the world.

There is an aspect of McCarthy's rhythm, on the other hand, which surrenders to that world. Whether or not their effects are natural to the novel, the rhythms of *The Road*, for all their grace, are not typical of prose. This in itself might be a source of winning lyricism or literary innovation. But there is a further problem. The deliberate artifice of McCarthy's rhythm functions not as resistance to nature, but as compliance. The efficient poetry that matches a waste world becomes, then, not ugly but wrong. In assiduously replicating the rhythms of that world, which is our world, *The Road* offers the false consolation of a naïve lyricism: sweet sounds instead of thought. At their best, McCarthy's names offer points of resistance, especially when they seem the narrator's rather than the man's words: they open up alternative universes, other ways of inhabiting this world. McCarthy's rhythm accepts the wasteland. In an interview, McCarthy noted his dislike for Marcel Proust and Henry James.[29] But one wonders—given such a world, what might their elaborate, speculative hypotaxis have done, what might they have written? The comparison suggests the possibility of prose rhythm as resistance, as an active force that questions and thinks.

Notes

1   See Alex Hunt and Martin M. Jacobsen, "Cormac McCarthy's *The Road* and Plato's Simile of the Sun," *Explicator* 66.3 (Spring 2008): 155–8.

2 We only hear the second emphasis, the contiguous stresses of *child sleep*-, because we have heard the first. Had McCarthy expanded his contraction, the triplets could have tripped on through the whole sentence: "he would reach out to touch the child sleeping beside him."

3 See George Monbiot, "Civilisation Ends with a Shutdown of Human Concern. Are We There Already?", *The Guardian* (30 October 2007); and Michael Chabon, "After the Apocalypse," *New York Review of Books* (15 February 2007).

4 "*The Road* Discussion Questions" <http://www.oprah.com/oprahsbookclub/Reading-Questions-Your-Guide-to-The-Road-by-Cormac-McCarthy/1> [accessed 10 October 2010].

5 John Jurgensen, "Hollywood's Favorite Cowboy," *Wall Street Journal* (20 November 2009); William Kennedy, "Left Behind," *New York Times* (8 October 2006).

6 Chabon suggests an especially ambitious mix of the novel and two poetic genres when he calls *The Road* "a lyrical epic of horror" ("After the Apocalypse"). Likening McCarthy's register to Yeats, Adam Mars-Jones praises *The Road* for "its poetic description of landscapes from which the possibility of poetry would seem to have been stripped"; see "Life After Armageddon," *Observer* (26 November 2006). In contrast, one reader calls McCarthy's style "just bad poetry formatted to exploit the lenient standards of modern prose"; see Louis Proyect, "Cormac McCarthy's 'muscular prose'" <http://louisproyect.wordpress.com/2008/02/13/cormac-mccarthys-muscular-prose/> [accessed 8 November 2010]. See, also, Joel Jacobson, "The Road by Cormac McCarthy" <http://jejacobson.wordpress.com/2010/01/26/the-road/> [accessed 10 October 2010].

7 Cormac McCarthy, *Blood Meridian* (1985; London: Picador, 1989), p. 3.

8 McCarthy, *Blood Meridian*, pp. 84, 118. For a consideration of intertextuality in *Blood Meridian*, see Amy Hungerford, "The American Novel Since 1945: Lecture 17" <http://oyc.yale.edu/english/american-novel-since-1945/content/transcripts/transcript-17-cormac-mccarthy-blood-meridian> [accessed 27 October 2010]. For thoughts on the judge and poetry, see Jay Twomey, "Tempting the Child: The Lyrical Madness of Cormac McCarthy's *Blood Meridian*," *The Southern Quarterly* 37.3–4 (Spring-Summer 1999): 255–65.

9 James Wood, "Getting to the End," *New Republic* (21 May 2007).

10 Richard J. Gray, "Open Doors, Closed Minds: American Prose Writing at a Time of Crisis," *American Literary History* 21.1 (Spring 2009): 128–48 (p. 136). John Cant makes a similar point in "*The Road*" (2008), in *Cormac McCarthy*, new edn, ed. H. Bloom (New York: Bloom's Literary Criticism, 2009), pp. 183–200 (p. 184).

11 Thus Wood continues: "When critics laud [McCarthy] for being biblical, they are hearing sounds that are more often than not merely antiquarian, a kind of vatic histrionic groping, in which the prose plumes itself up and flourishes an ostentatiously obsolete lexicon" ("Getting to the End").

12 In *The Orchard Keeper*, McCarthy describes the sky as "flickering like foil by half-light and gleaming lamely into shadow where it folded to the trees." Why "lamely"? For no other reason, Jay Ellis argues, than that it follows "gleaming" so "beautifully." If that's the only justification, it typifies the effects to which Wood objects, or what Ellis calls sound for sound's sake. See "McCarthy Music," in *Myth, Legend, Dust: Critical Responses to Cormac McCarthy*, ed. Rick Wallach (Manchester: Manchester University Press, 2000), pp. 157–70 (pp. 159–60).

13 William Hazlitt, "On the Prose-Style of Poets," in *The Complete Works of William Hazlitt*, ed. P. P. Howe, 21 vols (London: J. M. Dent, 1930–34), xii, 9.

14 I am thinking here, primarily, of the late nineteenth- and early twentieth-century flourishing of interest in English prose rhythm, represented perhaps most famously by Saintsbury. This interest was anchored by studies of clausulae and cursus in classical and mediaeval rhetorical theory. Much more recently, and with specific reference to McCarthy, Terri Witek has argued that his "strategy of rhythmic repetition becomes an integral part of the larger narrative structure," and so that rhythm serves "to order his plots," rhyming scene with scene. See "'He's Hell When He's Well': Cormac McCarthy's Rhyming Dictions," in *Myth, Legend, Dust*, ed. Wallach, pp. 78–88 (pp. 81–2).

15 Quintilian, *The Orator's Education*, trans. Donald A. Russell, Loeb Classical Library, 5 vols (Cambridge: Harvard University Press, 2001), 9.4.72. Quintilian does allow for the effective incorporation of parts of a line in some circumstances. Saintsbury echoes Quintilian's advice: "Verses or parts of verses, which present themselves to the ear as such, are strictly to be avoided in prose; but such as break themselves into prose adjustments are permissible, and even strengthen and sweeten the 'numerous' character very much"; see *A History of English Prose Rhythm* (London: Macmillan, 1912), p. 480.

16 Aristotle, *On Rhetoric: A Theory of Civic Discourse*, trans. George A. Kennedy, 2nd edn (New York: Oxford University Press, 2007), 3.8.1–3. Noting the effect of distracting prose rhythms, Longinus records that sometimes an audience, recognizing the too regular rhythms, would "beat time for the speaker and anticipate him in giving the step, just as in a dance"; see *On Sublimity*, 41.2, in D. A.

Russell and Michael Winterbottom, eds, *Classical Literary Criticism* (Oxford: Oxford University Press, 1989), p. 183.

17 George Gordon Byron, *Lord Byron: The Complete Poetical Works*, ed. J. J. McGann, 7 vols (Oxford: Clarendon Press, 1980–1993), iii, 309.

18 Hugh Kenner, *Ulysses*, rev. edn (Baltimore: The Johns Hopkins University Press, 1987), p. 34. More recently, Vincent J. Cheng has argued for Joyce's use of Anglo-Saxon meters; see "'The Twining Stresses, Two by Two': The Prosody of Joyce's Prose," *Modernism/modernity* 16.2 (April 2009): 391–9.

19 In the unlikely event that there is more than a metrical allusion here, McCarthy might be adapting James Russell Lowell: "The earth is full of music and delight, / But music formless, void of law or bound." See "The Power of Sound: A Rhymed Lecture," in *Uncollected Poems of James Russell Lowell*, ed. T. M. Smith (Philadelphia: University of Pennsylvania Press, 1950), pp. 110–26 (p. 113).

20 Aristotle, *On Rhetoric*, 3.8.4. Though he certainly advocates the classical scansion of English prose, Saintsbury rejects this attribution of fixed characters to different rhythms (*A History of English Prose Rhythm*, pp. 455–7).

21 Compare, for instance, Melville's *Mardi, and a Voyage Thither* (1849): "this same Hivohitee, whose name rumbled among the mountains like a peal of thunder." See Herman Melville, *Typee, Omoo, Mardi*, ed. G. Thomas Tanselle (New York: Library of America, 1982), p. 1018.

22 Though Dionysius of Halicarnassus recommends a mixture of short and long sentences, Saintsbury warns that an excessive "contraction and letting out, the constant sending forth giant and dwarf in company, communicates the smatch of cheap epigram" (*A History of English Prose Rhythm*, pp. 460–1).

23 Compare: "he woke in the darkness to hear something coming" (27); "He woke in the dark of the woods in the leaves shivering violently" (123; note the rhythmic "shiver" from rising to falling triplets); "He woke in the darkness, coughing softly" (299); and so forth.

24 Not to mention *sun* and *run-*, *black* and *vac-*, *-uum* and *un-*, *some* and *hunt-*. As ever, McCarthy's names mark the fall of civilization; those "blind dogs" are neither parhelia nor Helios' steeds.

25 Emerson is especially fond of the phrase "absolute truth." In "Self-Reliance," on which McCarthy's man might be said to rely, Emerson writes: "all persons have their moments of reason when, they look out into the region of absolute truth." See Ralph Waldo Emerson, *Essays & Lectures*, ed. J. Porte (New York: Library of America, 1983), p. 274.

26 This is quite unlike an earlier moment, when the man looks at the boy and fears "that something was gone that could not be put right again" (144). First, this seems a response to the horrors that the boy has seen on their journey, as if the boy has lost his innocence. Second, it may register the man's sense of an apocalypse, his feeling that the boy, who has only ever known this waste world, is lacking something of value from the lost world. But the repetition of the words on the novel's final page suggests that these thoughts are products of that more fundamental fall.

27 Plato, *The Republic*, 401d–2a. Compare *Protagoras*, 326a–b. See *The Complete Dialogues of Plato*, ed. E. Hamilton, H. Cairns, trans. Paul Shorey and W. K. C. Guthrie (Princeton: Princeton University Press, 1963).

28 Jurgensen, "Hollywood's Favorite Cowboy."

29 Richard B. Woodward, "Cormac McCarthy's Venomous Fiction," *New York Times* (19 April 1992).

4

Spring has lost its scent: Allegory, ruination, and suicidal melancholia in *The Road*

GRACE HELLYER

In *The Road*, an ambiguously represented event brings about the ruination of civilization and the elimination of almost all organic life. A father and son, referred to only as the man and the boy, traverse a landscape that is overwhelmed by the residue of a demolished past: the sky and ground are choked with "[t]he ashes of the late world" (10), every building is a ruin, and everywhere are dead trees and the corpses of "the mummied dead" (23). All objects have more or less shifted into the two categories of the useful and the redundant, with the overwhelming majority falling into the latter category, as the world "[shrinks] down about a raw core of parsible entities" (93). The other survivors that scrape out an existence on the "cauterized terrain" (13) of the new world exist in a "state of nature": violent conflict and absolute exploitation are represented as the basic conditions of interaction with other individuals. *The Road* represents a world in which the very structure of experience has changed such that the choice between survival and suicide has become particularly vexed. The question of suicide is linked to the improbability of avoiding a violent death, but also seems to hinge on a more subtle deformation of the category of experience.

The consciousness of the man is split between memories of the departed world and a present experience in which those memories no longer have any traction. The effects stemming from the loss of continuity between his past and present, and the subsequent attenuation of his experience can be usefully described using Walter Benjamin's concept of melancholia. Benjamin initially positions melancholia as a historically specific worldview that emerges in the baroque period, but he also frames it as a central category in his account of the decay of experience in modernity and the work of allegory as an artistic strategy that emerges out of and responds to these conditions. This essay will suggest that *The Road* puts forward allegory as a means of achieving a fragile intentionality that works to alleviate the suicidal despair of a melancholia that is ambiguously positioned between the consciousness of the man and the objective conditions of the new post-apocalyptic world.[1] In this account, the novel's theological references become melancholy traces manipulated by an allegorizing consciousness ambiguously positioned between the man and the narrator. In a world where the possibility of meaningful human existence has been radically diminished, indeed, all but extinguished, the work of this allegorizing consciousness is positioned as nothing less than a means of survival. The fragile constructions of allegory maintain both a distance and a means of engagement between the man and the boy, as well as a means of keeping faith with a world that no longer seems to offer any possibilities for the continuation of meaningful human life.

The destruction of the world of *The Road* is described only from the limited perspective of the man, so no cause or explanation is given. All that is described are "a long shear of light and then a series of low concussions" (54). Afterwards, the tenor of the man's experience seems always to retain a kind of congruence with this first series of unexplained and unexampled shocks. Although the existence of roads and his possession of a map allow him to plot a path across the burned-out continent, his progress remains marked by blindness and contingency: he and his son are always helplessly exposed to the next shock that lies in wait on the road, whether it is the sight of bodies twisted and mummified by blazing asphalt, a living man imprisoned and partially dismembered for consumption or the awful spectacle of a newborn infant roasting on a spit. The exposure of the man and boy to these constant shocks is combined with a curious quality of blankness in the man's experience. There is a tendency toward parataxis in the narration of the man's journey, which seems to be composed of a series of atomized moments that are lived through rather than being assimilated by an integrating consciousness. This is in contrast to the more rich and complex experiences that he retains as memories and dreams of the world before the apocalypse. This resonates with Benjamin's invocation of the attenuation of experience in the modern world. Benjamin begins his discussion of Baudelaire with the suggestion that the writer had to adjust his use of literary forms in order for his work to be "in rapport with the experience of its readers," and this, he suggests, "may [have been] due to a change in the structure of their experience."[2] Benjamin describes the kind of experience destroyed by modernity with reference to the poetic, the involuntary and the unconscious. It is anchored in tradition and ritual and composed of a convergence of diffuse and prolific sense data that is, for the most part, retained unconsciously. Its theorization is seen to arise as an almost unconscious reaction to the advent of a modernity that presents conditions under which it is unlikely to be generated. Benjamin regards modern experience as characterized by a constant succession of shocks. The subject of shock responds by maintaining a state of intense focus and alertness in order that the shock be "cushioned, parried by consciousness" and the organism protected from the trauma of its impact. While it would seem that the hyper-awareness induced by shock would intensify experience— "[lending] the incident that occasions it the character of having been lived in the strict sense"[3]—it in fact "sterilizes" the incident precisely by incorporating it into memory in a manner that is too directly conscious.

Intent on protecting his son, the man guards against dreams and recollections of the past, seeking instead to maintain a constant state of alertness. Minutely rendered and scrupulously attentive descriptions of the daily activities of the man and boy impart a sense of the man's terror of overlooking some detail crucial to survival:

He stood and warmed his hands inside his parka and then packed their shoes inside the knapsack along with the binoculars and the boy's trunk. He shook out the tarp and folded it and tied it with

the other blankets on top of the pack and shouldered it up and
then took a last look through the basket but that was it. (105)

When starvation or some other menace is imminent, the necessity of
maintaining a constant state of concentration and alertness is brought
into even more prominent relief: "he thought that he was getting stupid
and that his head wasn't working right. Concentrate, he said. You
have to think." (103) "He was going to cough. He put his whole mind
to holding it back" (120). It becomes a kind of a mantra for the man
to remind himself of the need to maintain a state of concentration;
to guard against involuntary physical and psychological impulses,
against the distractions of memory and the play of associations, and,
most importantly, against dreams of the past.

The Road begins with the man having woken from one of the
few dreams that seems to describe his present:

> In the dream from which he'd wakened he had wandered in a
> cave where the child led him by the hand. Their light playing
> over the wet flowstone walls. Like pilgrims in a fable swallowed
> up and lost among the inward parts of some granitic beast.
> Deep stone flues where the water dripped and sang. Tolling in
> silence the minutes of the earth and the hours and the days of
> it and the years without cease. Until they stood in a great stone
> room where lay a black and ancient lake. And on the far shore a
> creature that raised its dripping mouth from the rimstone pool
> and stared into the light with eyes dead white and sightless as
> the eggs of spiders. It swung its head low over the water as if to
> take the scent of what it could not see. Crouching there pale and
> naked and translucent, its alabaster bones cast up in shadow on
> the rocks behind it. Its bowels, its beating heart. The brain that
> pulsed in a dull glass bell. It swung its head from side to side and
> then gave out a low moan and turned and lurched away and
> loped soundlessly into the dark (1–2).

The creature seems to represent the conditions of life in the new
world in a nightmarishly exaggerated form. The immediate visibility
of its interior—not only of its bones, but also its brain, heart, and
bowels—creates an uncanny effect. While the creature's body is
translucent, its eyes are opaque, with this reversal suggesting a
fundamental deformation or inversion of the relationship of the

organism to its environment. The sensory disconnection of the creature from the external world is combined with an excessive exposure to it—a diminishing of the boundary between inside and outside. Thus, as is the case for the human inhabitants of the new world, an intensified susceptibility to physical shock is combined with a blunting of the sensory apparatus, a diminishment of the capacity for apprehension. The uncanny short circuit between inside and outside represented by the creature is reinforced by its being ambiguously linked with the physical environment of the man and boy in the dream. The apparition of the monstrous creature is anticipated by their being named as "pilgrims in a fable swallowed up and lost among the inward parts of some granitic beast." As the man and boy wander through this uncanny interior, the play of their light over the flowstone walls stands in opposition to the massive periods of time required for water to shape stone. In such conditions—physically vulnerable, disengaged from the external world, and totally stripped of agency—one can only wait for the inevitable wishing as the man does: "If only my heart were stone." (10)

The man's dream ushers in the world of *The Road* as one shaped by a melancholic view of human agency and history; one in which humans are subordinated to the massiveness of time and to a monolithic materiality in which they are irretrievably implicated and in the face of which they feel as if they must resign any sense of control over their fate. Benjamin discusses the effects of this bare awareness of the passage of time with reference to the motif of *spleen* in Baudelaire's *Les Fleurs du mal*. He finds the most devastating reference to this condition in the poet's declaration that "Spring, the Beloved, has lost its scent."[4] Scent is here associated with the complex and involuntary interconnection of sense data involved in that form of involuntary memory that, in Benjamin's thought is inseparable from authentic experience. *Spleen* is a state of mind that is opposed to the operation of involuntary memory, for it "musters the multitude of the seconds" against it, inducing a tense hyperawareness of the passage of time that blocks its unconscious operations:

In the spleen, time becomes palpable; the minutes cover a man like snowflakes. This time is outside history, as is that of the *mémoire involontaire*. But in the spleen the perception of time is supernaturally keen; every second finds consciousness ready to intercept its shock. (. . .) The spleen. . .exposes the passing moment in all its nakedness. To his horror, the melancholy man sees the earth revert to a mere state of nature. No breath of prehistory surrounds it: there is no aura (181–2).

Thus, when the poet declares that spring has lost its scent, he declares the devastation of individual consciousness and the destruction of memory. This loss corresponds with a loss of historicity and a subsequent loss of agency.

In the world of *The Road*, scent has become almost exclusively associated with the experience of shock. With the destruction of almost all organic life, there remains only the harshness of industrial smells, the reek of unwashed human bodies and of excrement, and of course the stench of dead bodies; there are very few positive references to olfactory experience. A rather poignant exception is one of the few instances in the book when the man and boy stumble on a "good place": a waterfall a little way off the road. The almost rapturous tactility of the man's response—"he squatted and scooped up a handful of stones and smelled them and let them fall clattering"—is inflected by a strange sense of absence. After he smells the stones, there follows a description that emphasizes their visually dazzling, jewel-like qualities—"Polished round and smooth as marbles or lozenges of stone veined and striped. Black disclets and bits of polished quartz all bright from the mist off the river" (38)—but does not include a description of their smell. The discovery of a "good place" seems to prompt a desire to imprint it as sense memory, and yet, one does not necessarily expect stones to smell, so the man's action registers as slightly eccentric—a kind of dislocated impulse directed at a lost reality that the waterfall points toward, but cannot really embody for him. In the same location, the man discovers a concealed clump of morels:

> A small colony of them, shrunken and dried and wrinkled. He picked one up and held it and sniffed it. He bit a piece from the edge and chewed.
> . . .
> Are they good?
> Take a bite.
> The boy smelled the mushroom and bit into it and stood chewing. He looked at his father. These are pretty good, he said (41).

Again, the act of smelling is described, but no description of the smell or, for that matter, the taste of the mushrooms is supplied though they are designated "good." This absence of detail is in contrast with the numerous occasions where the shock of an unpleasant smell is described: "the sour rank smell of the dead" (84); "Smell of mold and excrement"(114); "Rank odor" of ancient gasoline (141). The "good place" is supplied with a tactile description and the act of smelling is described, but no actual olfactory data is supplied. This culminates in the sensory sterility of the most comprehensively "good place" that the man and boy encounter: a bunker in which they are sealed away from the world and in which their food has been sealed away from the ravages of time in an abundance of cans. The eccentric relation of scent to memory and experience in the world of *The Road* also emerges when the man discovers a cistern "filled with water so sweet that he could smell it" (129). After he drinks, the thought surfaces that there is "[n]othing in his memory anywhere of anything so good" (30). Though in this case, the smell of the water is described, it causes the memory of the man to become blank rather than establishing correspondences with other memories.

Like the bunker filled with canned food, the waterfall is "a good place" (41), but the man refuses to stay there. He and the boy are compelled to continue on the road because of the impossibility of maintaining a defensive position in either location. It is probably this apparently unreasonable insistence on leaving a certain good in order to push ahead to the uncertain good of the coast that prompts the boy to ask after they have left the abundantly stocked bunker: "What are our long term goals?" (170). The father's inability to formulate such a goal is linked to the increasing indifference he feels in regard to the continuation of his own life. Even as he and his son enjoy a rare night of comfort and security in the bunker, the father confesses to himself that "[e]ven now, some part of him wished they'd never found this refuge. Some part of him always wished it to be over" (63).

The experience of the man can be characterized by Benjamin's conceptualization of *spleen*—"that feeling which responds to catastrophe in permanence"[5]—and is continuous with that quintessentially modern *weltschmerz* that Benjamin explores throughout his body of work. Benjamin's discussion of *spleen* is more or less continuous with his conceptualization of baroque melancholia as a set of aesthetic practices and, to a lesser extent, a psychological condition that emerges in response to the sense of loss associated with the de-centering of Christian hermeneutics and the subsequent draining of meaning from the material world. The link that I am describing between melancholia and the displacement of sense experience is very much in keeping with Susan Tyburski's discussion of the immanence of divine significance in sense experience and the opposition of this significatory fullness to suicidal despair in McCarthy's work. Tyburski hangs her argument on a phrase taken from McCarthy's play *The Sunset Limited*, where a character describes the role of God in his life in terms of scent—"if it aint got the lingerin scent of divinity to it then I aint interested." She argues that this association of "divinity" with scent dissociates the divine from reason, connecting it instead with "something more basic and elemental, even sensual."[6] The availability of this sensory experience of the divine is seen to be the only thing capable of preventing one of the protagonists of *The Sunset Limited* from giving way to a "suicidal impulse in the face of the meaninglessness of human existence" (121).[7] Tyburski's account of a suicidal despair brought about by the loss of "the scent of the divine" resonates with Benjamin's account of a baroque world in which meaning appears to have been drained away by the theological reconfiguration of the relation between material reality and the divine. This baroque worldview also characterizes the conditions under which the man lives. Although the theological concepts that shape his worldview no longer find any purchase on the world, his consciousness still carries the indelible and tragically displaced trace of religious belief. His responses to the landscape and to the people that traverse it constantly reiterate the absence of "God" as being at the heart of the loss that he has suffered. He tends to understand the horror of the blasted landscape in terms of it's being "godless" (2) and that of its inhabitants in terms of their being "creedless" (28). Christian metaphysics extend their imprint deeply into his consciousness, providing him with a fractured template through which to maintain a minimal engagement with an external world that has become hostile and alienated.

He rose and stood tottering in that cold autistic dark with his arms outheld for balance while the vestibular calculations in his skull cranked out their reckonings. An old chronicle. To seek out the upright. (. . .) Upright to what? Something nameless in the night, lode or matrix. To which he and the stars were common

satellite. Like the great pendulum in its rotunda scribing through
the long day movements of the universe of which you may say it
knows nothing and yet know it must. (14)

The invocation of autism in this passage is particularly interesting.
The transposition into objective terms of a subjectively experienced
detachment from external reality functions like Benjamin's
transformation of the "pathological" condition of melancholia into
an objective worldview. In this condition of externalized pathology,
the maintenance of even a fragile sense of agency becomes particularly
problematic. Here we see that the man's ability to orient himself
in relation to the landscape is premised not only on the existence
of a universal point of absolute stability, but also on the positing
of sentience in the universe—on a transcendent consciousness that
confers stability and movement on the heavenly bodies. The peculiar
mode of operation of this melancholy trace of Christian belief is
most apparent in the way in which the man conceives of his own
and his son's difference from the nameless others that scrape out a
bare existence on the denatured landscape. Scanning the horizon
for signs of life, he declares his son's difference as that trace of the
sacred word that will—like his quixotic push to the coast—give his
life a structure and a trajectory: "He knew only that the child was
his warrant. He said: If he is not the word of God God never spoke"
(3). As I will discuss later, this statement is of a piece with most of
the man's theological reflections, which—though they always seem
to be hovering on the brink of the revelation of some messianic
intentionality—always finally fall back on themselves.

As Samuel Weber points out, a fundamental aspect of the
worldview of baroque melancholia involves the loss of an eschato-
logical position from which to view and organize history:

> History as a repetitive and ineluctable process of rise and fall
> is identified with the nature of a fallen creation without any
> discernable, representable possibility of either grace or salvation.
> It is the loss of the eschatological perspective that renders the
> baroque conception of history "inauthentic" and akin to a state
> of nature.[8]

The Road represents a world that has uncannily continued to
exist beyond its own death, beyond the end of its own history.
Subsequently the novel both reinstates and hyperbolizes the

coordinates of precisely that loss of historicism that, for Benjamin, was a source of baroque melancholia. The man and the boy exist in a world that has fallen into the Real of history. The wife suggests as much when she refuses her husband's characterization of them as survivors and instead describes them as "the walking dead in a horror film" (57). In the promotional tagline of Romero's zombie classic *Dawn of the Dead* (1978), the living dead are said to issue from an overcrowded hell, the aimless emissaries of a world that is outside of history because it is beyond eschatology. It is in this sense that inhabitants of the post-apocalyptic world can be described as zombies rather than survivors. The man and boy exist in a space between life and death whose empty temporality operates as the horrifying excess of structured historical time.

This is a world in which, as Slavoj Žižek says of modernity in general, life has become "marked" in the sense that it "has to be especially motivated" (102) rather than being seen to possess an inherent, assumed value.[9] This denaturalization of life is brought into relief by the suicide of the wife, who, unable to bear the prospect of a violent death, cuts her own throat with a flake of obsidian. Randall S. Wilhelm describes the wife as bearing a "burden" of culpability, embodying as she does "the human mentality" that tends to "too readily relinquish the duty of life" (135).[10]

> As for me my only hope is eternal nothingness and I hope it with all my heart.
> He didnt answer.
> You have no argument because there is none.
> (. . .)
> And she was right. There was no argument. The hundred nights they'd sat up arguing the pros and cons of self destruction with the earnestness of philosophers chained to a madhouse wall (60).

I would add to this that the suicide of the wife signals the central problem of the novel—how to sustain life under conditions where the continuation of life can only be conceived of as a duty. The problem is not, as the man relates, that she forces him to realize that there is "no argument" for life, but the fact that she reveals that modern condition in which life requires an argument. Theodor W. Adorno has suggested that this may in fact be the argument that precedes all arguments. He raises the problem of suicide with reference to the statement of a character from a play of Sartre's:

> It is said by a young resistance fighter who is subjected to torture, who asks whether or why someone should live in a world in which one is beaten until one's bones are smashed. Since it concerns the possibility of any affirmation of life, this question cannot be evaded. And I would think that any thought which is not measured by this standard, which does not assimilate it theoretically, simply pushes aside at the outset that which thought should address – so that it really cannot be called a thought at all.[11]

It is the wife who brings this argument into focus, and while she bears the burden of representing the loss of life as a given, she also articulates a means of responding to this loss and sustaining the argument for life:

> The one thing I can tell you is that you wont survive for yourself. I know because I would never have come this far. A person who had no one would be well advised to cobble together some passable ghost. Breathe it into being and coax it along with words of love. Offer it each phantom crumb and shield it from harm with your body (59).[12]

The man's mistrust of the dreams of his wife as "the call of languor and of death" (7) implies a conscious unwillingness to employ such a strategy against loss. His apparent belief that the only possible responses to loss are a suicidal attachment to the lost object or the assertion of complete detachment from it evokes Freud's original distinction between mourning and melancholia, where mourning is a process that follows the loss of a loved object, and melancholia represents a pathological deviation from that process. In "Mourning and Melancholia," he argues that the loss of the object establishes a tension between a will to live that is premised on the total detachment of libido from the object, and a desire to follow the object into death. Normal mourning is understood as a kind of work in which "great expense of time and cathetic energy" is devoted to the withdrawal of libido from all memories and expectations attached to the lost object. The end of this work is an ego that is "free and uninhibited" and able to fully direct itself toward the future discovery of new objects in which to invest the libido.[13]

Unlike the suicidal indifference of the kid in *Blood Meridian*, which Guillemin discusses as symptomatic of his "melancholy psychosis," the mother's suicidal indifference is, technically speaking, the most rational position represented in *The Road*. In the post-apocalyptic world of the novel, a fundamental reversal has taken place so that it is the "normal" psychology of mourning that has become perverse. With the world being swiftly emptied of its objects, it has become far more rational to "cobble together some passable ghost" (59) than to anticipate the arrival of a new object in which to invest the libido, more rational even to choose suicide over the inevitable prospect of starvation or violent death. As empirical observation reveals a reality that is actually illumined by the black sun of melancholy, *The Road* could be seen as set in a world where the melancholic disposition has become both rational and realistic: a valid worldview. Subsequently, the mother's suggestion that constructing a ghost should operate as a means of keeping suicidal indifference at bay, reveals itself as a survival strategy of the melancholic consciousness that is more sustaining than the mere survivalism of the man. It is thus that *The Road* puts forward allegory as a melancholic labor pitted against the suicidal despair that Tyburski has identified as central to McCarthy's late work. Allegory offers a means of interacting with reality that is undercut by a sense of the loss of the meaningful totality conferred by Christian hermeneutics, while at the same time offering a means of engaging with the world.[14]

Fredric Jameson describes allegory as "the painful attempt to restore a continuity to heterogeneous, disconnected instants."[15] Such an attempt can be identified in the elegantly economical dialogues between the man and the boy. Often, there is a ritualistic quality to their exchanges: a sense that they have nothing to say and are speaking as a sort of duty to one another. The dialogues tend to consist of a series of questions and answers in which it is obvious that both parties already know the answers to the questions. Their function seems to be to affirm, and sometimes to probe or evaluate the possibility of a shared and purposive trajectory of whose existence neither the man nor the boy seem even minimally certain:

Are we going to die?
Sometime. Not now.
And we're still going south.

Yes.
So we'll be warm.
Yes.
Okay.
Okay what?
Nothing. Just okay. (9)

The hollow affirmative, "okay," interminably repeated throughout the narrative, can be said to function allegorically in that it ostentatiously fails to denote a definite referent while still operating so as to keep the possibility of dialogue and engagement open. Rather than signifying agreement, the "okay" operates as a truce in the only marginally articulated struggle between the man and the boy, a stand-in for the absence of a stable agreement between them. It is the delicate, dialogic maintenance of this simultaneous accord and disagreement that eventually enables the boy's emergence as a distinct entity capable of principled opposition to his father.

The work of allegory becomes more ambiguous in the man's private contemplation of his son, where he manifests an unnerving tendency to describe him as if he were actually an incarnation of the godhead, evoking that paradigmatic example of the theological dimension of the symbol—Christ. The tension between allegory and symbol in the man's thought can be described with reference to Benjamin's development of the concept of allegory through a critique of the theological dimension of the romantic symbol:

> The unity of the material and the transcendental object, which constitutes the paradox of the theological symbol, is distorted into a relationship between appearance and essence. The introduction of this distorted conception of the symbol into aesthetics was a romantic and destructive extravagance which preceded the desolation of modern art criticism.[16]

An ambiguous intent often seems to hover around the habitual use of religious imagery by the man in his contemplation of the boy as beautiful image: the emergence of a will to impose the sacred on the formless ruin of the world by regarding the boy in a way that invokes the romantic notion of the perfect individual in whom transcendental ideas of moral truth and beauty are immanent.[17] His devotion to his son blurs into a religious awe that occasionally takes on the aspect of a statement of intention as when he describes him as a "[g]olden chalice, good to house a god" (178). The man never gives voice to this line of thought in the presence of the boy, though when they share a meal with an elderly vagrant named Ely, the man asks him—"what if I said that he's a god?" (183). Nevertheless, there is a distinct and crucial tension maintained in the representation of the man's pseudo-theological thought, one that is borne out in Benjamin's distinction between symbol and allegory. As Jameson puts it in his discussion of Benjamin's work on the *Trauerspiel*: "[t]he distinction between symbol and allegory is that between a complete reconciliation between object and spirit and a mere will to such a reconciliation."[18]

A certain tension between completely embracing allegory and retaining a furtive investment in the efficacy of the symbol is typical of the *Trauerspiel*. Lutz T. Koepnick points out that baroque drama often "subterraneously...reproduces the complicity of tragedy with myth," ultimately revealing a final hesitation to fully and finally embrace a completely secularized worldview.[19] Thus, in the face of "transcendental hopelessness [and] melancholic despair," the baroque sovereign will be represented as desperately invoking "mythic residues" in an attempt to ground his faltering sense of authority.[20] This is the case in *The Road* when the man seeks to justify decisive courses of action directed against the external world by using the boy as symbolic mandate. The boy becomes the man's justification for denying aid to other vulnerable individuals encountered on the road, for killing a man whom he regards as a threat to the boy, and for stripping a thief of all his possessions and clothes and leaving him for dead. Throughout the narrative, the boy's objection to the way in which his father grounds these decisions becomes increasingly explicit. Initially the ghost of a disagreement will only emerge elliptically, typically through repetition or a refusal to speak:

And we couldnt help them because then they'd eat us too.
Yes.
And that's why we couldnt help them.
Yes.
Okay (135).

Toward the end of the narrative, the initially almost exclusive representation of the boy through the melancholy consciousness of the father becomes fractured as the boy begins to assert a degree of disagreement with or difference from his father with increasing frequency and explicitness. This crucial shift takes place almost exclusively through their sparse and deceptively apathetic dialogues. The becoming apparent of this initially submerged process of subjectification, manifested in one case through the boy's explicit objection to the man's contemplation of him ("Stop watching me," 205), subtly displaces the man's construction of the boy as symbol by drawing attention to its nature as a construction.

Even the man's references to "carrying the fire," which seem to operate as an invocation of some quasi-theological ground for his rudimentary moral system, are inflected by the way that fire operates elsewhere in the man's rhetoric. In the following passage, in which the man wakes to see a fire blazing along a ridge, the link between fire and the sun describes a trajectory from a sense of a past plenitude to a present sense of loss.

> Everything was alight. As if the lost sun were returning at last. . . . Cold as it was he stood there a long time. The color of it moved something in him long forgotten. Make a list. Recite a litany. Remember (31).

In this passage, the fire's appearance as palliative for the lost sun performs the function of stimulating memory and the impulse to memorialize even as it gestures toward that ubiquitous destitution that structures the narrative. The visual splendor of the fire serves as a simultaneous denial and reminder of loss and as a call to an ongoing labor of memory—the work of melancholic consciousness. The notion that "fire" as a theological reference operates as an ultimate ground for the moral standards of the man and boy ignores the manner in which it operates elsewhere in the man's rhetoric: as a fragile allegorical construction against an irreducible and final loss.

Finally, just as fire provides a palliative for the loss of the sun, so the generation of quasi religious rituals in relation to the boy becomes part of the means by which the man is able to keep the infinite sadness of melancholia at bay. The man's construction of rituals is often explicitly positioned against the ritual's ultimate ungroundedness:

He watched him stoke the flames. God's own firedrake. The sparks rushed upward and died in the starless dark. Not all dying words are true and this blessing is no less real for being shorn of its ground (31).

He kicked holes in the sand for the boys hips and shoulders. All of this like some ancient anointing. So be it. Evoke the forms. Where you've nothing else construct ceremonies out of the air and breathe upon them (78).

Thus, although it seems to denote an investment in the symbol in its quasi theological dimension, the man's worshipful stewardship of the boy is ultimately described in terms of a ritual that always reveals its nature as a melancholic allegorical construction against suicidal despair. Although the man's pseudo-theological thinking resounds through the narrative, the novel is structured around the displacement of the theological worldview and its negative imprint in the landscape of a blasted world.

Notes

1 For an excellent analysis of the operation of the melancholic constellation of allegory, subjective destitution, and infanticide in McCarthy's early work, see Georg Guillemin's *The Pastoral Vision of Cormac McCarthy* (College Station: Texas A&M University Press, 2004). Louis Palmer's reading of *The Road* through the lens of mourning and the elegiac also operates along similar lines to Guillemin's, though he privileges Freud's rather than Benjamin's concept of melancholia. See Palmer, "Full Circle: *The Road* Rewrites *The Orchard Keeper*," *The Cormac McCarthy Journal*, Vol. 6 (Autumn, 2008), pp. 62–9.

2 Walter Benjamin, in *Illuminations*, trans. Harry Zohn (London: Fontana Press, 1973), p. 158. Here, Benjamin draws a distinction between two German words for experience: *Erfahrung*, which is dependent on tradition and is capable of being assimilated by the integrating consciousness of the subject, and *Erlebnis*, which is associated with *spleen* and with the shocks of modernity. *Erlebnis* is more or less indigestible to consciousness and is merely lived through, inducing a state of alienation and disempowerment in the subject.

3 Benjamin, "On Some Motifs in Baudelaire," p. 158.

4 Benjamin, "On Some Motifs in Baudelaire," p. 180.

5 Walter Benjamin, "Central Park," trans. Lloyd Spencer and Mark Harrington, *New German Critique*, 34 (Winter, 1985), p. 34.

6 Susan Tyburski, "'The Lingering Scent of Divinity' in *The Sunset Limited* and *The Road*," *The Cormac McCarthy Journal*, 6 (Autumn 2008): 121.

7 Tyburski bears these symbolic coordinates into her discussion of *The Road*, though she does not refer to its representation of olfactory experience in the novel. Instead, she focuses on its representation of darkness and impaired vision and links this degradation of visual experience with the man's suicidal despair, a despair alleviated only by his investment in the safety of the boy in whom the "scent of divinity" resides.

8 Samuel Weber, "Taking Exception to Decision: Walter Benjamin and Carl Schmitt," *Diacritics*, 22.3/4, Commemorating Walter Benjamin (Autumn–Winter, 1992), p. 9.

9 Slavoj Žižek, *On Belief* (London and New York: Routledge, 2001), p. 102.

10 Randal S. Wilhelm, "'Golden Chalice, Good to House a God': Still Life in *The Road*," *The Cormac McCarthy Journal*, 6 (Autumn, 2008): 135.

11 Theodor W. Adorno, *Metaphysics: Concept and Problems*, ed. R. Tiedemann, trans. Edmund Jephcott (Oxford: Polity Press, 2000). p. 111.

12 Benjamin explicitly links ghosts with allegories because both "are manifestations from the realm of mourning; they have an affinity for mourners, for those who ponder over signs and over the future." Walter Benjamin, *The Origins of German Tragic Drama* trans.) George Steiner (London & New York: Verso, 1998), p. 108.

13 Sigmund Freud, "Mourning and Melancholia," trans. James Strachey, *The Standard Edition of the Complete Psychological Works of Sigmund Freud*, Vol. XIV (London: Vintage, The Hogarth Press and The Institute of Psychoanalysis, 1957), p. 245. This ruthlessly progressivist view of the ego is, as Tammy Clewel points out, softened in Freud's later works where the internalization of, and identification with, the lost object is conceived of as central to identity formation.

14 Ilit Ferber frames Benjamin's transformation of melancholia from a pathology to a worldview as a specific kind of challenge to Freud's distinction between the normalcy of mourning and the deviation of melancholia. For Freud, melancholia entails the stalling of the work of mourning. It is this hitch in the normal labor of maintaining an autonomous ego that effects the internalization of the lost object. This invasion of the subject by the object causes the ego to become divided against itself and subsequently, to become self-destructive. In contrast,

Benjamin imports a concept of work into the melancholic framework, such that the melancholic response to the loss of the object becomes associated with the presentation of loss, rather than its disavowal. Subsequently, both the work of art and the work of creating concepts create a means of interacting meaningfully with the world, without relying on a false notion of absolute certainty because forms like the allegory, the fragment and the "constellation" allow for the incorporation of loss in their presentation of the object. Thus, allegory as the work of melancholy consciousness (*Trauer-arbeit* as Ferber puts it) is a means of achieving a fragile intentionality that puts a border around the infinite sadness of the melancholic. Ferber, "Melancholy Philosophy: Freud and Benjamin," *Numéro* 4.1 (2006): 66.

15   Fredric Jameson, *Marxism and Form: Twentieth Century Dialectical Theories of Literature* (Princeton, New Jersey: Princeton University Press, 1971), p. 72.

16   Benjamin, *Origins*, p. 160.

17   p. 32–58. For Benjamin, the romantic construction of the symbol was a "destructive extravagance" inasmuch as it presupposed "the unlimited immanence of the moral world in the world of beauty." He finds the groundwork of this construction in classicism, "in the tendency to the apotheosis in the individual who is perfect, in more than an ethical sense. . ..." The romantics, in turn, tend to place this Christ-like individual within a redemptive progression of events that strives to attain the sacred (Benjamin, 1928, 160). Although this seems to resonate with the way that the boy is represented, I want to suggest that the man's "romantic" construction of the boy wavers between symbol and allegory and is eventually displaced by the boy's emergence as a distinct entity.

18   Jameson, *Marxism and Form*, p. 72.

19   Lutz P. Koepnick, "The Spectacle, the 'Trauerspiel', and the Politics of Resolution: Benjamin reading the Baroque Reading Weimar," *Critical Inquiry*, 22.2 (Winter, 1996): 280.

20   Benjamin, *Origins*, p. 80.

5

The late world of Cormac McCarthy

MARK STEVEN

On this road there are no godspoke men. They are gone
and I am left and they have taken with them the world.
Query: how does the never to be differ from the
never that was? (32)

Animals without world

"I hold that we are at a very special moment," writes Alain Badiou: "a moment *at which there is not any world*."[1] The critical freight of this declaration is borne by its immediacy. Rather than prophesying an end to come, Badiou insists categorically that the present is singular in its actualization of something apocalyptic. Sibylline scriptures foretelling this "worldless" moment litter the shelves of philosophy, theology, and literature; before turning their way, however, I want to situate its phenomenal epicenter on American soil by aligning my interpretation with the geopolitical thrust of Fredric Jameson's assessment of postmodernism. For Jameson, "this global, yet American, postmodern culture is the internal and superstructural expression of a whole new wave of American military and economic domination throughout the world: in this sense," he argues, "as throughout class history, the underside of culture is blood, torture, death, and terror."[2] Writing more recently, Slavoj Žižek claims that the real "danger" of this worldwide expression is that "although it is global, encompassing all worlds, it sustains a *stricto sensu* 'worldless' ideological constellation, depriving the great majority of people of any meaningful 'cognitive mapping.'"[3] Badiou and Žižek have taken Jameson's account of postmodernism to the limit. From their standpoint, the victory of globalism in its current formation has resulted in the ontological attenuation of its individual subjects. Marching in step to the war-drums of capital, flanked by the banners of liberal democracy, a postmodern empire has catalyzed the nonexistence of any unified "world."

But what can this mean, that there is no longer any world? Here Badiou elaborates his axiomatic into the beginnings of a disquisition:

> In its circumstantial aspect, capitalist nihilism has reached the stage of the non-existence of any world. Yes, today there is no world as such, only some singular and disjointed situations. No world exists simply because the majority of the planet's inhabitants today do not even have a label, a simple label. . . . Today, outside of the grand and petty bourgeoisie of imperial cities who proclaim to be 'civilization,' there is only the anonymous excluded. 'Excluded' is the name for those who have no name, just as 'market' is the name for a world that is not a world.[4]

Our moment lacks its world because the splintered shards of meaningful existence have ceased to register within a globalized, superstructural expression. Now, "the planet's inhabitants" and the cultural worlds they would otherwise inhabit slip through the desiccated syntax of "postmodernism" and into the lexical grid of the "market," recodifying as the homogenized biomass of (what Žižek calls) a "neutral economico-symbolic machine."[5] This is what Badiou is referring to as our "worldlessness."

With this chapter I argue that on the pages of Cormac McCarthy's apocalypse novel, *The Road*, the cultural logic of worldlessness is first allegorized in narrative and then turned back against itself in generic form and characterology. In view of the qualifications expressed below, my claim will be that *The Road* has something very significant to offer its readers: if not the literary construction of a new "world" then the presentation of that world's lineaments. In this book, whose narrative is set against the blasted topography of North America, an ontological chiasmus plays out around two protagonists—the unnamed "man" and his son, the "boy"—as they tramp for months through cinders and toward the blackened sea. "They plodded on," we read, "thin and filthy as street addicts. Cowled in their blankets against the cold and their breath smoking, shuffling though the black and silky drifts." (188) Here the survivors of some undisclosed event have all been stripped of their labels, evacuated from the global nomenclature, and so it is that North America has become a pronominal echo chamber wherein the anonymous multitude is returned to the imperial city now in ruins.

But first, and to set the stakes for such a reading, I should like to begin by considering worldlessness in tandem with a philosophical discourse on animalism, taking my cue from *The Road*'s exquisite final passage:

> Once there were brook trout in the streams in the mountains. You could see them standing in the amber current where the white edges of their fins wimpled softly in the flow. They smelled of moss in your hand. Polished and muscular and torsional. On their backs were vermiculate patterns that were maps of the world in its becoming. Maps and mazes. Of a thing which could not be put back. Not be made right again. In the deep glens where they lived all things were older than man and they hummed of mystery. (306–7)

As it was for William Blake ("To see a world in a grain of sand. . ."[6]), here world is distilled into that space between the sublimely infinite and the immaculately particular. Narrative perception rapidly shifts from the "streams in the mountains" to the "amber current" and then to the "white edges of their fins," as though it is driven down by the gravitational descent of one cosmic zoom, to finally settle over the "vermiculate patterns" on the trout's backs, which under close inspection reflect the mysterious expanse of an unknown future: "maps of the world in its becoming. Maps and mazes." To hold the promise of universal truth alongside its particularity in the palm of one hand is to live with an abundance of being. It would be, in Badiou's schematization, to "seize hold of the discontinuous variety of worlds and the interlacing of objects under the constantly variable regimes of their appearances."[7] But that promise is rescinded and those "worlds" have been stolen away: the remembered trout refer only to "a thing which could not be put back. Not be made right again."

Now try to imagine how a grizzly bear would set itself upon McCarthy's brook trout. Standing waist deep in the stream, transfixed in sensing somewhere beyond its own aqueous reflection, it discerns only the fleet, muscular movement of the trout; then finally, at long last, it drives one paw down with preternatural force, half-crushing the other animal beneath it. The instinctual myopia that would propel such behavior is what constitutes the animal's "encirclement" or "disinhibiting ring," its failure to perceive those greater "maps of the world in its becoming," and such is the logic by whose permit Martin Heidegger once announced with certainty that the beast is "poor in world."[8] Here is what he had to say:

> Every animal as animal has a specific set of relationship to its sources of nourishment, its prey, its enemies, its sexual mates, and so on. . . . The animal's *way of being*, which we call '*life*,' is *not without access* to what is around it and about it, to that amongst which it appears as a living being. It is because of this that the claim arises that the animal has an environmental world of its own within which it moves. Throughout the course of its life the animal is confined to its environmental world, immured as it were within a fixed sphere that is incapable of further expansion or contraction.[9]

It was Jacques Derrida who glossed Heidegger's thesis in psychoanalytic terms, claiming that the animal "always has a relation of utility, of putting-in-perspective; it doesn't let the thing be what it is, appear as such without a project guided by a narrow 'sphere' of drives, of desires."[10] Of all philosophers, Derrida is only keenest to suggest that this ontological circumscription now pertains to humans just as it did to Heidegger's animal; and so, when he insists that "[t]he *first* and *decisive* question will rather be to know whether animals *can suffer*," we should already know the answer.[11] Putting weight behind that terminal emphasis, Derrida seems to have addressed his own provocation several years earlier, in *Specters of Marx* (1993), at "a time when some [had] the audacity to neo-evangelize in the name of the idea of a liberal democracy that has finally realized itself as the ideal of human history:

> never have violence, inequality, exclusion, famine, and thus economic oppression affected as many human beings in the

history of the earth and of humanity . . . let us never neglect this obvious macroscopic fact, made up of innumerable singular sites of suffering: no degree of progress allows one to ignore that never before, in absolute figures, have so many men, women and children been subjugated, starved or exterminated on the earth.[12]

Such is the abyssal vortex into which we have descended as one collective planetary phylum: the members of our fortunate minority are born into the "disinhibiting rings" of a worldless market; and, for the fatally unfortunate majority excluded from that market, there is only the "encirclement" of immeasurable suffering. Perhaps it is because of the foreseeable synchronicity between these two breeds of animal-human that Derrida chose to add the following strange comment to his thoughts on the geopolitical class divide, though only in parentheses: "we must leave aside here the nevertheless indissociable question of what is becoming of the so-called 'animal' life, the life and the existence of 'animals' in this story. This question," he claims, "has always been a serious one, but it will become massively unavoidable."[13] The question has indeed become unavoidable; and McCarthy, as I now want to show, has made no attempt to avoid it.

In *The Road*, the division between animal life and human life has receded, leaving the biological descendants of humankind to stand, by day, "in the rain like farm animals" and, by night, to lay down either "shivering like a dog" or to "sleep under the tree like some hibernating animal." (20, 69, 103) As though having fallen in solidarity with McCarthy's quadrupeds ("the saltbleached ribcages of what may have been cattle," 182) a host of aviary and oceanic creatures are simply dumped in heaps along waterside America. "The bones of seabirds," describes the narrator, "the ribs of fishes in their millions stretching along the shore as far as eye could see like an isocline of death. One vast salt sepulchre." (237) McCarthy's ocular simile extends a cruelly absolute message to what remains of this pitiful species of ours, for it doubles one type of animal-humanism with the other, uniting both before the horizon of zoomorphic extinction. The man's wife is aware of the ontological miscegenation afoot here and so forewarns of their family's death sentence before her own suicide. "Sooner or later they will catch us and they will kill us," she says. "They will rape me. They'll rape him. They are going to rape us and kill us and eat us and you wont face it." (58)

This precariously extant strain of animal-humanism has appeared in political thought bearing the ancient mark of the *homo sacer*, a sign which refers specifically to those men, women, and children for whom "there is no autonomous space within the political order of the nation-state," that sovereign zone from within which they are excluded.[14] Here, for instance, the man and boy identify themselves with the transient and anonymous figure of the refugee:

> I think we should take a look. If it's a commune they'll have barricades. But it may just be refugees.
> Like us.
> Yes. Like us. (82)

And, from earlier in the book, the only other appearance of that noun:

> In those first years the roads were peopled with refugees shrouded up in their clothing. Wearing masks and goggles, sitting in their rags by the side of the road like ruined aviators. Their barrows heaped with shoddy. Towing wagons or carts. Their eyes bright in their skulls. Creedless shells of men tottering down the causeways like migrants in a feverland. (28)

Unless they have already been assimilated into one of the novel's militarized hordes, every character in *The Road* has come to typify a multitude whose very existence negates that of a world because of its isolated members' exclusion from "the originary spatialization that governs and makes possible every localization and every territorialization."[15] If these ideological "localizations" and those geopolitical "territorializations" constitute the "disinhibiting ring" of a postmodern worldlessness, what will characterize the *homo sacer* is its exclusion from that ring. Debarred by and from globalism, however, *homines sacri* are redefined by the successive force of what Agamben calls their "double exclusion," wherein life is exposed to extreme violence in a way that "is classifiable neither as sacrifice nor as homicide, neither as the execution of a condemnation to death nor as sacrilege."[16] And again, the man and his wife in conversation:

We're survivors he told her across the flame of the lamp.
Survivors? she said.
Yes.
What in God's name are you talking about? We're not survivors.
We're the walking dead in a horror film. (57)

McCarthy's blighted landscape offers only death. These characters
are biologically alive but symbolically dead; their lives mean nothing
and so their bodies can be destroyed without reproach. And around
them, after the apocalyptic consumption of all sovereign orders,
the embolic clots of "civilization" are transformed into bands of
murderers who localize the toll of a global holocaust by impaling
their dead on spikes along the road.

"He'd seen it all before," thinks the man when presented with
an abject corollary of all this. "Shapes of dried blood in the stubble
grass and gray coils of viscera where the slain had been field-dressed
and hauled away. The wall beyond held a frieze of human heads,
all faced alike, dried and caved with their taut grins and shrunken
eyes." (94) Surely this image is an echo of the palisade surrounding
Kurtz's station in *Heart of Darkness* (1899). "The round knobs
were not ornamental but symbolic," we read in that book: "they
were expressive and puzzling, striking and disturbing—food for
thought and also for the vultures if there had been any looking
down from the sky. . ."[17] The allusion will be of consequence here
but only if we recall the primordial shadow to which Marlow, the
narrator, attributes these decapitated heads:

They only showed that Mr Kurtz lacked restraint in the
gratification of his various lusts, that there was something
wanting in him—some small matter which, when the pressing
need arose, could not be found under his magnificent eloquence.
Whether he knew of this deficiency himself I can't say. I think
the knowledge came to him at last—only at very last. But the
wilderness had found him out early, and had taken on him
a terrible vengeance for the fantastic invasion. I think it had
whispered to him things about himself which he did not know,
things of which he had no conception till he took counsel with
this great solitude—and the whisper had proved irresistibly
fascinating. It echoed loudly within him because he was hollow
at the core . . .[18]

What I take McCarthy's tableau to signify, then, is the animal-human's entry into the disavowed "wilderness" of secular biopolitics. "The heads not truncheoned shapeless had been flayed of their skins," we read, "and the raw skulls painted and signed across the forehead in a scrawl and one white bone skull had the plate sutures etched carefully in ink like a blueprint for assembly." (95) This cranial "blueprint" is an inversion of the "maps" we are yet to encounter with McCarthy's brook trout, preemptively occluding the future their "vermiculate patterns" would have otherwise promised. And so, having entered the arena of the *homo sacer*, the animal-human's "solitude" brings it face to face with the negative imprint of a world that is not: the "hollow core" of worldlessness.

But, given McCarthy's emphasis here on the production of meaning, I wonder if these cenotaphic stakes might also mark the pegging out of an earth upon which we can begin the construction a new world: a world that is, for a psyche structured by the symbolic injunctions of late capitalism and for an imagination so evidently predisposed against anything like a "commune" or "community," an unthinkable utopia of the highest order. It is a utopia whose seeds inhere throughout the genetic code of the animal-humanism that has been brought here under the operation of prose, for if the human is animal then surely the animal must also be human, or at least retain something like human immanence; and indeed, by transforming characters into refugees, expelling them from the "disinhibiting rings" of globalism, their immanent capacity to form a world might once again be actualized. McCarthy, however, refuses to commit this improbable vision to narrative. His late world is witheringly stretched across the axes of hostility and fear. He casts his characters back into the bestial "encirclements" of omnipresent violence, which Julian Murphet in this volume describes as their degeneration from *homo sapiens* into *homo homini lupens*. "People sitting on the sidewalk in the dawn half immolate and smoking in their clothes," reads one passage. "Like failed sectarian suicides. Others would come to help them. Within a year there were fires on the ridges and deranged chanting. The screams of the murdered." (32–3) The political allegory is demystifying and perhaps even illuminating; but, to risk putting it cruelly, doesn't all of this simply read as an emblazoned performance of its author's own bad faith? Perhaps we are not yet ready to ask of McCarthy's book the question of a new world.

Genre and event

Scholars of post-apocalyptic literature never tire of pointing out that the end is never really the end; what the fictional apocalypse actually drives into their variform death throes are "a way of life, a configuration of attitudes, and a system of beliefs."[19] The lesson we should carry away from this generic conjunction is fairly straightforward: if contemporary life, attitudes, and beliefs all comprise a postmodern expression of the worldless, then an apocalypse would surely consume that expression as well as its determinate technologies. Building upon this relatively simple hypothesis, allow me to conjecture that generically post-apocalyptic fiction fashions textual spaces that are open to the possibility of ontological clarity and, perhaps, to the distillation of a new world. Here Agamben provides an account of how such fiction might read when he compares the characters of Robert Walser's literary oeuvre to

> the freed convict in Kafka's *Penal Colony*, who has survived the destruction of the machine that was to have executed him, these beings [who] have left the world of guilt and justice behind them: The light that rains down on them is that irreparable light of the dawn following the *novissima dies* of judgment. But the life that begins on earth after the last day is simply human life.[20]

What is generic about *The Road* is the passage it constructs around "the last day" and its attempt to posit a kind of "simple human life" thereafter. We shall do well to understand the formal mechanics of this arrangement.

McCarthy's apocalypse takes the form of a cataclysmic "event," but one whose impact appears to have been dulled between phenomenal irruption and sensory perception. "The clocks stopped at 1:17. A long sheer of light and then a series of low concussions," and then, several sentences later: "A dull rose glow in the windowglass." (54) This understated sketch, which is the only description we are ever provided with, tessellates with Badiou's idea that an event "can only be *thought* by anticipating its abstract form, and it can only be *revealed* in the retroaction of an interventional practice which is itself entirely thought through."[21] The apocalypse can only exist in anticipation and retroaction, before and after, whereby the latter actualizes something utterly unimaginable from within the former;

and, because of this, it has no readily appreciable present. The man's pregnant wife, "cradling her belly in one hand," questions him twice only to be met with the most insubstantial of replies: "What is it? she said. He didnt answer" and again "What is it? she said. What is happening? I dont know." (54) Here apocalypse resounds to the very core of Badiou's philosophical project, illustratively giving depth and dimension to a unique kind of phenomenon that might totally shatter the coordinates of a worldless "market" by energizing the nameless essence of its "void." Badiou reasons that the event is either

> in the situation, and it ruptures the site's being 'on the-the-edge-of-the-void' by interposing itself between itself and the void; or, it is not in the situation, and its power of nomination is solely addressed, if it is addressed of 'something,' to the void itself.[22]

The meaning of "void" is crucial, for it designates not just an absence of molecular matter (a "lack") but also the inconsistent and hitherto imperceptible being within a given situation; and it is such being, returned here to the site of literature, that is made unmistakably apparent and unforgivingly present by the transformative force of the event. "The ashes of the late world carried on the bleak and temporal winds to and fro in the void," we read only a few pages in. "Carried forth and scattered and carried forth again. Everything uncoupled from its shoring. Unsupported in the ashen air. Sustained by a breath, trembling and brief." (10) The apocalypse happens between the worldless man's situation and its void, forging an interpositional bridge between the two, and so it disperses into his lifeworld everything that had been repressed and de-nominated from within the distributional matrix of late capitalism.

If postmodernism is formally manifest as a kind of "internal and superstructural expression," then it must be significant that McCarthy's event ruptures the symbolic order of the sign itself, rending asunder the atomic particles of language, de- and re-coupling the base materials of practical world-formation as well as postmodern expression:

> The names of things slowly following those things into oblivion. Colors. The names of birds. Things to eat. Finally the names of things one believed to be true. More fragile than he would have

thought. How much was gone already? The sacred idiom shorn of its referents and so of its reality. Drawing down like something trying to preserve heat. In time to wink out forever. (93)

The void presents itself as a kind of paradox: its advent names the unnamable as unnamed and so brings to light from implacable darkness the disintegration of a world whose destruction McCarthy has already made literal. But for McCarthy to annihilate the world it must first be written or "named" into being. Here the "names of things" follow their referents "into oblivion"; but, as they go, these signs light up one last time before "winking out" forever in that final celestial dance. What fail to produce this combustive heat of denotation, however, are "the names of things one believed to be true." The loosely held convictions that define our historical situation are exposed as lacking the material coordinates from which to assemble any sort of "cognitive map" or "world." There go the "market" and its "fragile" abstractions, passing away silently and unmourned, to wane beyond the twilight of their own reckoning. This selectively efflorescent prose is either typical of the post-apocalyptic genre or it speaks to a presupposed generic ideal; but, given its exemplarily precise realization under McCarthy's skilled hand, the particular sense I have of it here is that what we are encountering may in fact be the calculated retrieval of certain nouns from the wasteland of postmodern expression. The idea that McCarthy has created a system of positive differentiation, a literary apparatus that separates the threads of a world tapestry ("Colors. The names of birds. Things to eat.") from those of a postmodern non-world, originates in the book's management of its own language. It should also be demonstrated, however, that this system has issued down from the macroscopic field of its genre.

"As soon as genre announces itself," Derrida once took up that compositional law, "one must respect a norm, one must not cross a line of demarcation, one must not risk impurity, anomaly or monstrosity."[23] Consider in light of this point the malformed creature that McCarthy describes in his opening paragraph: "Crouching there pale and naked and translucent, its alabaster bones cast up in shadow on the rocks behind it. Its bowels, its beating heart. The brain that pulsed in a dull glass bell." (2) The post-apocalyptic genre ought to contain nothing but a world or earth that no longer exists or, precisely, nothing at all; but what it really contains is a monstrous concatenation that appears to have metastasized here in ghastly prosopopeia. So much about McCarthy's creature speaks to its own immersion in a slow and inescapable death; and yet, if we take into account the concentration of verbal energy emanating off of its body, it begins to resemble one of Alberto Giacometti's frail animal sculptures, with every molecule bristling with animate life. This is how the genre sires images of itself. Thus, if I am once again nearing Agamben's phrase ("the life that begins on earth after the last day is simply human life") it is only because the generic laws upon which a properly post-apocalyptic book and its metatextual spawn would be predicated are, as Derrida has it, utterly inseparable from "a principle of contamination, a law of impurity, a parasitical economy."[24]

What I want to add here is that the morphological contaminants reinscribing an apocalyptic death with new life are themselves novelized symptoms, corresponding to the disavowed spaces and the subjugated masses that comprise the void in our own historical situation. Indeed, and to stay with this creature for just one more paragraph, that much should be inferred from the as yet uncited allusion McCarthy seems to be striving for with his opening figure. Tempting though it may be to comparatively cite the "rough beast" of William Butler Yeats, "its hour come round at last," or even to conjure up an image of Plato's shadowy cave, I take McCarthy's creature as a more direct allusion to Osip Mandelstam's allegorical poem, "The Age," (1923) whose first stanza reads:

> My age, my beast, who will be able
> To look into your pupils
> And with his own blood glue together
> The vertebrae of two centuries?
> Blood-the-builder gushes
> From the throat of earthly things,
> Only a parasite trembles
> On the threshold of new days.[25]

Trembling with Mallarméan intensity here is the unborn "new" as it kicks hard from within the womb of the old. "Perhaps in the world's destruction it would be possible at last to see how it was made," writes McCarthy near the end of his book. "Oceans, mountains. The ponderous counterspectacle of things ceasing to be. The sweeping waste, hydroptic and coldly secular. The silence." (293) What the centrality of McCarthy's uncommon adjective ("hydroptic") would imply, however, is that a new world might still cry out despite the crushing silence of its protracted gravity. And so reads the first quatrain of Mandelstam's third stanza:

> In order to pull the age out of captivity,
> In order to begin a new world,
> The elbows of nodular days
> Must be bound with a flute.[26]

That the "new world" is ushered in with a flute is imperative to our reading of McCarthy. As Badiou has it, "there is only the flute of art. Without a doubt this is the principle of courage that underlies any cognitive enterprise: to be of one's time, through an unprecedented manner of not being in one's time."[27] Perhaps this is why, in one of *The Road*'s most touching moments, the man carves for his son "a flute from a piece of roadside cane. The boy took it wordlessly," we read. "After a while he fell back and after a while the man could hear him playing." And what the man hears is precisely what we should be listening for in McCarthy's prose: "A formless music for the age to come. Or perhaps the last music on earth called up from out of the ashes of its ruin." (81)

The unimaginable

But how are we to listen for a music that is properly formless and how is it that we will know such music when we hear it? Recall Arnold Schoenberg's "Wind Quintet" of 1924 and Krzysztof Penderecki's "Fonogrammi" of 1961: two marvelous flute-songs "for an age to come," but it is an age which for them was unrealized just as for us it has already passed. Turning away from these problematically precedent citations, then, it will not be the language of musicology that provides the coordinates for the answer I have in mind but the conceptual framework of psychoanalysis. In the writings of Jacques Lacan, "Real" is the name given to an order of the psyche that resists symbolic and imaginary form: in no straightforward way can it be integrated into syntactical code or visual representation. The Real is manifest in *The Road* when natural matter is accounted for in prose that is by even measures sensuous and sensibly indeterminate. In one such instance, the man "laved up a handful of [water] and smelled and tasted it and then drank. He lay there a long time, lifting up the water to his mouth a palmful at a time. Nothing in his memory anywhere of anything so good." (129–30) Such weirdly evaluative description with its purely verbal accentuation of touch, smell, and taste marks a movement from sensible reality to something that is accounted for neither within the structures of an established language nor by the sedimented images of the man's memory. Another attestation of the Real is encountered at its most extreme as a human harvest when the man and boy stumble into the basement of an ostensibly abandoned house:

> On a mattress lay a man with his legs gone to the hip and the stumps of them blackened and burnt. The smell was hideous.
> Jesus, he whispered.
> Then one by one they turned and blinked in the pitiful light. Help us, they whispered. Please help us. (116)

This is horror at its most abject. For McCarthy, the Real has converted itself into irremediably shocking environs and it will do so again as the man and boy are forced to "pick their way among the mummied figures. The black skin stretched upon the bones and their faces split and shrunken on their skulls." (204) Now consider the frozen immobility implied by the next simile and its discordant relationship with the dynamism of the sentence to follow: "Like victims of some ghastly envacuming. Passing them in silence down that silent corridor through the drifting ash where they struggled forever in the road's cold coagulate." (204) This presentation, whose signifying elements generate not a composite image made up of multiple shocks but a singular something far more harrowing than the sum of its individual parts, is brilliantly contradictory. It invites only "silence," a muting of the symbolic, for there are no words equipped to register the affective disquietude of this dislocated passageway. Like the basement, it too is Real.

If what we have encountered here is not the "formless music for an age to come" but, rather, a masterful attempt to arraign both the insensible and the traumatic in prose, then let us stake a wager with Žižek, for whom there is not one but three modalities of the Real. And here, allow me to suggest that what we should

be reading in pursuit of is the "imaginary-Real," which he defines
as the "unfathomable something on account of which the sublime
dimension shines through an ordinary object."[28] As with worlds, the
imaginary-Real comprises an interwoven matrix of particulars held
together by "the fragile, pure appearance" of a singular figure; and
so, to describe it as an effect of this "ordinary object" to which we
have direct access (the book), my own prose will inevitably become
an index to its formlessness: to be sure, the closer we get to the
imaginary-Real the more speculative, conditional, and subjunctive
my expression will have to be in order to capture something of its
essence. Recall the book's final sentence, composed in melancholy
anamnesis: "In the deep glens where they lived all things were
older than man and they hummed of mystery." (307) That barely
remembered sound, the epiphenomenal hum of creation, is what I
have in mind when thinking of this ineffable sublimity.[29] To revivify
the imaginary-Real from within the dead letters of contemporary
American literature would be to align postmodern expression with
its "unfathomable" other: here we might even envisage an utterly
compromised "economico-symbolic machine" on the terrestrial
collision course of (to steal another of Žižek's phrases) a "cultural-
symbolic world."[30]

   But I wonder if McCarthy is capable of engineering this feat of
imagination. Moments before death, for instance, the man observes
his son "standing there in the road looking back at him from some
unimaginable future, glowing in that waste like a tabernacle."
(231) This figural vision is familiar in its inconceivability, that
narratological denial of the imaginary, for it echoes the penultimate
paragraph from McCarthy's own *Outer Dark* (1968), an incest
story modeled on the gothic plots of William Faulkner:

   Late in the day the road brought him into a swamp. And that was
   all. Before him stretched a spectral waste out of which reared
   only the naked trees in attitudes of agony and dimly hominoid
   like figures in a landscape of the damned. A faintly smoking
   garden of the dead that tended away to the earth's curve. He
   tried his foot in the mire before him and it rose in a vulvate
   welt claggy and sucking. He stepped back. A stale wind blew
   from this desolation and the marsh reeds and black ferns among
   which he stood clashed softly like things chained. He wondered
   why a road should come to such a place.[31]

From McCarthy's standpoint, any attempt to move beyond what already is, to pursue the imaginary-Real, will be to crawl back into some impubescent fantasy zone. It is a grotesque fantasy presented in this earlier novel as the forbidden return to the kindred maiden's open vagina, "a vulvate welt claggy and sucking," the geographical contours of which have evolved out into the primeval swamp of all regressive nightmares. It is not to be wondered, then, why the boy's future is "unimaginable." McCarthy, it seems, cannot bring himself to render in prose that mysterious, unfathomable community of a coming world, the shimmering light of an imaginary-Real, now intertextually aligned with the unthinkable object of exogamous taboo. Instead, he writes and rewrites the symptomatic nexus of its other two manifestations, sublating energy from that singularly repressed modality into the fervent attention he so evidently dedicates to what Žižek would call the "symbolic-" and the "real-Reals," the insensible and the traumatic.[32] This is McCarthy's apocalypse, the way he works the genre, writing his way around an unimaginable lacuna. For all its style and grandeur, The Road is an exemplarily powerful rendition of these generic coordinates; but, to regain focus and pursue a question whose answer now refracts through the optic of an imaginary-Real: does this book lay claim to something like a new world?

"Okay"

Saint John the Divine:

> And I looked, and behold a pale horse: and his name that sat on him was Death, and Hell followed with him. And power was given unto them over the fourth part of the earth, to kill with sword, and with hunger, and with death, and with the beasts of earth.[33]

A hoary man calling himself Ely, somewhere along the road:

> When we're all gone at last then there'll be nobody here but death and his days will be numbered too. He'll be out in the road there with nothing to do and nobody to do it to. He'll say: Where did everybody go? And that's how it will be. What's wrong with that? (184)

With precious few exceptions, it is a merely graphic depiction of death that appears on the horizon of all generic apocalypse narratives today. What I want to conclude with, however, is a detailed argument that *The Road* is one of those exceptions and that its historical as well as its literary significance will ultimately derive from the way its characters respond to the event therein. But before that and for the sake of conceptual clarity, allow me to press down on Badiou's claim that the animal-human's becoming human and reclaiming its world is contingent upon its response to an event. "There is only a particular kind of animal," he writes,

> convoked by certain circumstances to *become* a subject—or, rather, to enter into the composing of subject. This is to say that at a given moment, everything he is—his body, his abilities—is called upon to enable the passing of a truth along its path. This is when the human animal is convoked to be the immortal that he was not yet.[34]

Only the embodied assertion of an event's truth—manifest in the void that it exposed—is what can restore a lost world. When the animal-human internalizes the demystified actuality of its situation, its body will have become an agent for truth, and that truth will only manifest in the agent's transformation of the evental site in accord with its pursuit; and, if the pursuit of truth therefore drives the animal-human into an otherwise "unimaginable future," then we can say that this convocation of being will have restored its humanity, obliterating its animalism, even if only in the singular instance. "Subjectivization," writes Badiou, "aporetic knot of a name in excess of an un-known operation, is what *traces*, in the situation, the becoming multiple of the true, starting from the non-existent point in which the event convokes the void and interposes itself between the void and itself."[35] If the subjective return to humanity "traces" the proliferation of truth, the tying together of signs and objects in and out of the void and all under the tangled appearance of a world, then its place in literature will already be known to us, for its name is "character," a nominal quilting point of history and form. Could it be possible, then, that McCarthy's book presents something like a truth-procedure, potentially elevating this quest for a world to an all-important question of character?

As *The Road*'s only free indirect discourse belongs to the father, we have no real access to the boy's thoughts. Despite or even because of this, however, it becomes possible to locate an isomorphic convergence between what the boy's laconic diction ostensibly signifies and the rhetorical structures of its signifying syntax as well as the lexical choices made therein. If world is ontology manifest within the symbolic, an imaginary-Real immanent to a language of names, then such a convergence would open a space from which we might argue the boy wields a unique capacity to articulate a world. Recall the semantic and thus literary dimension to *The Road*'s void: "The names of things slowly following those things into oblivion. . . . The sacred idiom shorn of its referents and so of its reality." (93) While so many material referents have been irrevocably destroyed, the boy's spoken language molds their ashes into something like that which Agamben evokes in his discussion of "the irreparable": "After the judgment," he writes, "animals, plants, things, all the elements and creatures of the world, having completed their theological task, would then enjoy an incorruptible fallenness—above them floats something like a profane halo."[36] In the boy's appositely sparse vocabulary, this binding irreparability finds form nowhere so ably than with the hauntingly pervasive term, "okay," itself a profanely lexical halo that comes to hover over all things worthy of being.

If "okay" designates acceptability and thus acceptance, then perhaps this term will stand as the rhetorical embodiment of the first step in Badiou's convocation in being, maybe even distinguishing the internalization of an irreducible truth. Here the man defines this term as the internalization of that which simply is:

That's the best deal you're going to get.
Okay.
Okay means okay. It doesnt mean we negotiate another deal tomorrow.
What's negotiate?
It means talk about it some more and come up with some other deal. There is no other deal. This is it.
Okay.
Okay. (175–6)

His father's definition illuminates the semantic potential of "okay" as it is realized within the boy's lexicon as a response to McCarthy's wrought devastation. The subject of an event, Badiou has written, "cannot *make a language* out of anything except combinations of the supernumerary name of the event and the language of the situation," and that is what "okay" appears to have become: a recognizable lexeme whose semantic transfiguration refers itself as an indexical sign to humanity's overcoming its worldless animalism.[37] For the boy, the meaning of "okay" evolves along two distinct axes: vertically, it binds certain referents to their own irreparable existence after the event, naming them into semantic subsistence; and horizontally, it draws these referents together into a network of mutually contingent signifieds, all of which are held together by the flux of polysemy. The referents, to be sure, present themselves in language as the following signifieds: the mortal fragility of bodies (9, 98, 105); an eternity without Coca Cola (23) and without automobiles (44); unconditional forgiveness (53 56, 200, 262, 278, 285); existential uncertainty (81, 196); perseverance and persistence (62, 92, 143, 145, 209, 289, 299); a tin of peaches (148) and the combination of butter and biscuits (154); giving thanks for peaches, pears, butter, biscuits, and shelter (155); the abandonment of personal property (169); the movements of fellow travelers, both friendly and hostile (135, 170, 171, 205, 303, 304); an old abandoned house (218); the disfigurement of the ocean (230); the possibility of life elsewhere, on the other side of that ocean (231); paternal and filial fidelity (249, 260, 264, 299); and, finally, the right to drink when thirsty (267). So much being is held together here by a single word, the very scintilla of meaning, as it is uttered over and over again in the mouth of a child.

It is thus that the word "okay" generates via its multiple combinations and deliberate reiterations a uniquely complex stylistic profile under whose nominal precinct we shall find those final referents out of which the subject is to construct a world: an awareness of one's own body in relation to the bodies of others, all of which are so evidently bound together and potentially energized by a combinatorial ethos of forgiveness, fidelity, faith, and fortitude. That is how the boy appears in relation to McCarthy's narrative event: he affirms the reality of the void, but he also allows it to direct his being toward a truth whose actualization will utterly transform its situation. And perhaps it is because of how unfamiliar the boy's potential really is that he is compared to a magical deity, whose invisible operations would likewise conjoin the word and the body, the form and its figure, from some unimaginable beyond: "If he is not the word of God," says the man near the book's beginning, "God never spoke" (3); and, from a new character, at the book's end: "the breath of God was his breath," she says, "yet though it pass from man to man through all of time." (306) What the beatific evocations speak to here is not mere spiritual hyperbole, but to the boy's characterological immortality, which extends far beyond his role in McCarthy's narrative.[38] My claim is that a response to the event from within *The Road* is significant for reasons that are both historical and literary. In closing I should like to think about the boy in relation to each of those two fields.

Historically speaking, McCarthy writes as though he is attuned to this "very special moment" of ours at which the "economico-symbolic machine" of late capitalism has all but obliterated the "cultural-symbolic world." The consequences of the resultant "worldlessness" include a regressive process of global de-nomination, which is manifest in the proliferation of the *homines sacri* and the *homo homini lupens* whose fictional avatars populate *The Road*. It is, to be sure, with the term "okay" that the boy draws the *homo sacer* closer to himself, for to be "okay" is to not only recognize others but to commit that recognition to action. Here, after the boy has convinced his father to offer an old man some of their provisions, "okay" begins to grind with interpersonal dissonance:

> The man watched him. Are you talking? he said.
> Yes. But you're not happy.
> I'm okay.
> When we're out of food you'll have more time to think about it.
> The boy didnt answer. They ate. He looked back up the road. After a while he said: I know. But I wont remember it the way you do.
> Probably not.
> I didnt say you were wrong.
> Even if you thought it.
> It's okay.
> Yeah, the man said. Well. There's not a lot of good news on the road. In times like these.
> You shouldnt make fun of him.

Okay.
He's going to die.
I know. (185–6)

Note the repeated vocalization of "okay," first and second by the boy and third by the man; and note, also, the shifts in the man's tone (there are two, from interrogatory to accusing, and from accusing to accepting, each heralded by the boy's utterance): it is as though the boy's breath passes through the man, momentarily transforming him so that, in the closing three lines, their perspectives finally converge. With this simultaneously phatic and deictic term the boy has devised a signifier with which to designate the void of a planet that has been ruined entirely, naming into the anonymous elect those shards of life once excluded from the imperial city and those earthly objects on which they shall subsist. What all of this denotes, then, is that the boy has reacted against his father's individualistic and libertarian survivalism to the point of internalizing an idea of community, a community that comprises the irreparable everyone and everything of a ruined earth: starving beggars (51; 171–8), mutilated thieves (273–6), companion animals severed of company (86, 91), and orphaned children (89–90), all of whom the boy wishes to assemble together by the power of the word; and indeed, we should call this a world. Yet if it really is a world, which we cannot know for certain, it is necessarily blocked from our view by an absence of recognizable names. Perhaps this is why, in what I read as the book's most agonizing moment, the boy cannot "name" his dead father into their narrative space but only repeat the abstract noun: "When he came back he knelt beside his father and held his cold hand and said his name over and over again." (301)

If it is the boy who, in good dialogic style, opens McCarthy's novel to "a great multitude, which no man could number, of all nations, and kindreds, and people, and tongues,"[39] returned here in the leveling gesture of an apocalypse; and if it is the boy's internalization of the multitude via a "sacred idiom" of irreparability that finally delivers an ontological plenitude from within the book, then the device upon which all of this is sustained, the literary character as such, will have to be my final point of comment. The book's defining treatment of what is inside the boy's head, of what would make up his subjective disposition but which here is the substance of his character, is given over only when the man and his son enter "a country where firestorms had passed," now peopled with "the dead. Figures half mired in the blacktop, clutching themselves, mouths howling." (203). That infernal site yields the following conversation:

> Take my hand, he said. I dont think you should see this.
> What you put in your head is there forever?
> Yes.
> It's okay Papa.
> It's okay?
> They're already there.
> I dont want you to look.
> They'll still be there.
> He stopped and leaned on the cart. He looked down the road and he looked at the boy. So strangely untroubled. (203)

This fragment of dialogue comes closest in all of the book to revealing the boy's characterology from within itself, an instance of his own self-reflexive sense of being-in-the-world, for it is here that he defines "okay" in terms of a unique potential for generating a "cognitive map" out of all things made forever internal. The boy, therefore, is of particular significance within the tradition of American letters, as his character marks the return of an older, seemingly abandoned form of literary subjectivity, a "self" first committed to paper in 1855, revised continuously up until 1881, and which has not been celebrated anywhere quite so ably since:

> Do I contradict myself?
> Very well then I contradict myself,
> (I am large, I contain multitudes.)[40]

And, from the same pen but a few pages earlier:

> In all people I see myself, none more and not one a barley-corn less,
> And the good or bad I say of myself I say of them.
> I know I am solid and sound,
> To me the converging objects of the universe perpetually flow,
> All are written to me, and I must get what the writing means.[41]

It is from the chiasmic immanence of these nameless "multitudes" and "converging objects," all of which cohere together in the boy's imagination as world, that "the sublime dimension shines through an ordinary object." If the literary significance of *The Road* will proceed from its tracing this older make of character, from its inscribing the barest delineation of Walt Whitman's ontology within the field of contemporary prose, then the instructional difference between each of these forms will be in their perspective: Whitman's lyrical-I is now McCarthy's semi-omniscient narration, a voice that has exteriorized the world of a characterological interior to which we have been denied access by the unsparing axiomatics of late capitalism. The necessity which drives this shift is that, unlike Whitman who knowingly lived in an ecologically integrated world and willfully named everything, the man and McCarthy both recognize that the power to conceive of a world and to name anything might be something truly otherworldly for a consciousness bled dry; and so it remains intramural within the boy as he maps an historical void actualized by literary event:

> Maybe he understood for the first time that to the boy he was himself an alien. A being from a planet that no longer existed. The tales of which were suspect. He could not construct for the child's pleasure the world he'd lost without constructing the loss as well and he thought perhaps the child had known this better than he. He tried to remember the dream but he could not. All that was left was the feeling of it. He thought perhaps they'd come to warn him. Of what? That he could not enkindle in the heart of the child what was ashes in his own. (163)

Notes

1 Alain Badiou, "The Caesura of Nihilism," *Poiesis: A Journal of the Arts and Communication* 6 (2004): 183, original emphasis.
2 Fredric Jameson, *Postmodernism: Or, the Cultural Logic of Late Capitalism* (London & New York: Verso, 1991), 5.
3 Slavoj Žižek, *The Parallax View* (Cambridge, MA: MIT Press, 2006), 318. Cognitive mapping refers to a mental process whereby the subject acquires, retains, and decodes information about various phenomena within a metaphorical spatial environment. See Jameson, *Postmodernism*, 44–5.

4 Badiou, *Polemics*, trans. Steve Corcoran (London & New York: Verso, 2006), 34.

5 Žižek, *The Parallax View*, 318.

6 William Blake, *The Complete Poetry and Prose of William Blake*, ed. D. V. Erdman (New York: Anchor Books, 1988), 490.

7 Badiou, *Logics of Worlds*, trans. Alberto Toscano (London: Continuum, 2009), 1.

8 Martin Heidegger, *The Fundamental Concepts of Metaphysics: World, Finitude, Solitude*, trans. William McNeill and Nicholas Walker (Indiana: Indiana University press, 1995), 196.

9 Heidegger, *The Fundamental Concepts of Metaphysics*, 198, original emphases.

10 Jacques Derrida, *The Animal That Therefore I Am*, trans. David Wills (New York: Fordham University Press, 2008), 159. See, for a Marxist perspective, Badiou, *Logics of Worlds*, 2; and, for a theological perspective, Giorgio Agamben *The Open: Man and Animal*, trans. Kevin Attell (Stanford: Stanford University Press, 2004).

11 Derrida, *The Animal That Therefore I Am*, 27, original emphases.

12 Derrida, *Specters of Marx: The State of Debt, the Work of Mourning and the New International*, trans. Peggy Kamuf (London & New York: Routledge, 1993), 106.

13 Derrida, *Specters of Marx*, 106.

14 Agamben, "We Refugees," trans. Michael Rocke, *Symposia* 42.2 (Summer 1994): 117. See the essays by Paul Sheehan and Julian Murphet in this volume.

15 Agamben, *Homo Sacer: Sovereign Power and Bare Life* trans. Daniel Heller-Roazen (Stanford: Stanford University Press, 1998), 111.

16 Agamben, *Homo Sacer*, 82–3.

17 Joseph Conrad, *Heart of Darkness*, ed. R. Hampson (London & New York: Penguin, 2007), 71.

18 Conrad, *Heart of Darkness*, 72.

19 See, for instance, James Berger, *After the End: Representations of Post-Apocalypse* (Minnesota: University of Minnesota Press, 1999), 26; Eric S. Rabkin, *The End of the World* (Carbondale: Southern Illinois University Press, 1983), 1–2; David Seed, *Imagining Apocalypse: Studies in Cultural Crisis* (Houndmills, Basingstoke, Hampshire: Palgrave, 2000), 52. Quoted is Rabkin.

20 Agamben, *The Coming Community*, trans. Michael Hardt (Minneapolis: University of Minnesota Press, 1993), 6–7.

21 Badiou, *Being and Event*, trans. Oliver Feltham (London: Continuum, 2005), 178, original emphases.

22 Badiou, *Being and Event*, 182.
23 Derrida, "The Law of Genre," in *Modern Genre Theory*, ed. D. Duff (London: Pearson Education Limited, 2000), 221.
24 Derrida, "The Law of Genre," 224.
25 Osip Mandelstam, trans. Steven Bryode, quoted in Badiou, *The Century*, trans. Alberto Toscano (Cambridge: Polity, 2007), 12.
26 Mandelstam in Badiou, *The Century*, 13.
27 Badiou, *The Century*, 21.
28 Žižek, *For They Know Not What They Do: Enjoyment as a Political Factor* (London & New York: Verso, 2008), xii.
29 This effect is different to the earthquakes that reverberate through the novel on two separate occasions (28, 279). The key difference is that, while the epiphenomenal "hum" is bound to a sense of futurity, these purely phenomenal tremors signify extinction.
30 Žižek, *The Parallax View*, 318.
31 McCarthy, *Outer Dark* (New York: Random House, 1968), 242.
32 Žižek, *For They Know Not What They Do*, xii.
33 *The Bible: Authorized King James Version*, ed. R. Carrol, S. Prickett (London & New York: Oxford University Press, 1997), 304.
34 Badiou, *Ethics: An Essay on the Understanding of Evil*, trans. Peter Hallward (London & New York: Verso, 2006), 40, original emphasis.
35 Badiou, *Being and Event*, 394.
36 Agamben, *The Coming Community*, 39.
37 Badiou, *Being and Event*, 396.
38 A productive comparison could be made here between the boy and the similarly Christological figure of Joe Christmas from Faulkner's *Light in August* (1932), a novel from which McCarthy is known to have borrowed plot devices and images. Like the boy, Christmas is presented as an elusive exterior, about whose psychical interior and genetic composition the other characters can only speculate.
39 *The Bible*, 305.
40 Walt Whitman, *Leaves of Grass and Other Writings*, ed. M. Moon (London & New York: Norton, 2002), 77.
41 Whitman, *Leaves of Grass*, 42.

6

Road, fire, trees: Cormac McCarthy's post-America

PAUL SHEEHAN

Twenty years ago, Richard Rorty issued what might now be seen as a kind of mission statement, a distillation of his philosophical itinerary. In *Contingency, Irony, and Solidarity* (1989), he offered a detailed profile of his model intellectual, the "liberal ironist," and described the sort of utopian social conditions in which this person could prosper. "A postmetaphysical culture," he wrote, "seems to me no more impossible than a postreligious one, and equally desirable."[1] As with Nietzsche, one of his (non-liberal) ironist archetypes, Rorty believed metaphysics and religion to be so deeply entwined that social and cultural reform could only begin when *both* had been successfully routed. His "cure" for America's over-investment in religious faith was, coming from a philosopher, both surprising and (as it turned out) prescient: "narrative redescription," the rewriting of relationships, attitudes, beliefs, and life-experiences, in a bid for human solidarity. Further, Rorty stipulated that of all the narrative genres, it was the novel that could be most effective in terms of initiating social improvement, citing Dickens, Proust, Henry James, Orwell and Nabokov as exemplars. The novel, he declared, along with the movies and television, had "gradually but steadily, replaced the sermon and the treatise as the principal vehicles of moral change and progress" (xvi).

For anyone sympathetic to Rorty's position, or looking for some sign of his "ironist utopia," or just wishing that America would get over its religious hangover, the reception accorded Cormac McCarthy's *The Road* cannot but be disheartening. A novel that redescribes American achievement as so much cultural and industrial detritus, and exposes communal bonds as (at best) a cover for naked self-interest, nevertheless brought to the fore some tendentious and rarefied commentaries. Beguiled by the book's post-apocalyptic premise and quasi-biblical narrative voice (not unique in the McCarthy oeuvre, as it happens), a number of critics have seen the book as a eulogy to spiritual fortitude and the tenacity of belief.

Some of these critics examine the book's themes in broadly religious terms. Robert Elder, for example, considers the work to be a testament to Christian Truth, hence counterposed to the "godless morality" of Richard Dawkins, Christopher Hitchens, et al.[2] In a similar vein, Lee Brewer Jones notes that the novel "draw[s] inspiration from the New Testament" and that "it looks at the bleaker elements in the Revelation."[3] Others, however, regard the text as a more *specific* engagement with Christian ideas, even at the level of plot. So for Carl James Grindley, the novel is "a document of the so-called Tribulation of Judeo-Christian mythology,"[4] and for Thomas H. Schaub the book's narration is a form of "secular scripture," and the man and the boy's journey a quest for the sacred that invokes "the promise of Christian redemption."[5] Equally as fervent is Thomas A. Carlson, who reads the work through Augustine's notion of "worldly time," in which "the genuine future is closed out by the deadly recurrence of sin" and diminished memory and expectation "recall, as in another perverse imitation, the eternity of Augustine's otherworldly God."[6]

I wish to argue, by contrast, that although there is a surfeit of religious allusions filling out the interstices of the novel, the questions they raise concerning faith and belief acquire a more critically directed *political* orientation as the narrative unfolds. However, this is not to countenance—in another wrongheaded view—any reading that gives priority to the politics of climate change. The most enthusiastic advocate for this view is the writer and political activist George Monbiot, who, with unashamed hyperbole, describes *The Road* as "the most important environmental book ever written" that "will change the way you see the world."[7] That may indeed by the case, but it is also true that eco-conscious jeremiads tend to provide endless hypothetical detail of the scientific-meteorological events that will ensue as a result of climate change. McCarthy, by contrast, makes no attempt to represent, apportion blame for, or even just *name* the disaster that has ravaged the world. This reluctance effectively transforms the book from a warning (as Monbiot would have it) into an outcome, where effects are of greater import than causes.

But if *The Road* does have a serious political agenda, as I am claiming, it is also the case that McCarthy seems determined to distract his readers from arriving at it too hastily. In the first place, the drama he is staging turns on the notion of "bare life." Even just to invoke this term, without any context, is to summon allusions to a juridical order, and to a form of life conceived of by law, subject to state power and control, and defined by "its capacity to be killed."[8] McCarthy's bare life, by contrast, is something more austere and elemental—life outside of organized social and political machinations, not *Homo sacer* but *Homo vivere*. And in depicting human beings as subject not to juridical decrees but to biospheric collapse, McCarthy poses a simple question: how much can be pared away from human existence for it still to qualify as "life"?

A still more instructive contrast can be made with a (superficially) similar work: Michael Haneke's 2004 film, *Le Temps du loup*. As in *The Road*, a mysterious catastrophe has led to generalized societal breakdown, forcing human beings to flee the cities and seek sustainability in the country. Like McCarthy, Haneke not only refuses to portray the catastrophic event, he also withholds discussion of it among his characters. In addition, sinister religious undercurrents infiltrate the survivalists' discourse; there is a boy, not unlike McCarthy's, devoted to self-sacrifice; and rumors abound of a mythical train, signifying potential deliverance (paralleling the distant promise of salvation for the man and the boy as they journey toward the coast). Yet the points of divergence are, if anything, even more striking. Haneke puts his (fatherless) family into situations that involve incipient communal groupings and rudimentary forms of self-governance, hinting at how social alliances congeal to form power structures. McCarthy's (motherless) family, by contrast, seeks to minimize contact with others, evading social interaction wherever possible ("[W]e dont like for people to stop" [170], the man tells the boy). Though glimpses are provided of two menacing, itinerant "collectives" on the lookout for potential prey—the "roadagents" (gangs of marauders) and the "blood-cults" (armies of marching men with slaves and catamites in tow)—there is no question of the protagonists being recruited to or assimilated by either group.

Yet despite these "impediments," there is an imposing political agenda at work in *The Road*, that shines an unflattering light on America's present-day troubles. As Richard Gray notes, McCarthy is confronting the "ghosts that haunt the twenty-first century, particularly in the West and especially in America," and in doing so has devised strategies "to address contemporary pain, offering a realistic measure of its extraordinary scope, the sense of apocalypse that now seems to haunt the West."[9] Following Gray's lead, I propose to examine the nature of these "ghosts," by showing how the aforementioned religious material is eclipsed by more pressing contemporary political concerns. And in doing so, I will explore the hinterland between civilization and barbarism, the fraught space where *The Road* mostly takes place, and through which McCarthy seeks to diagnose the current malaise of the West.

The problem of the worst

Global economic turmoil and ominous environmental forecasts have thus far defined the political landscape of the new century. These two crises are taking place, however, against a backdrop that some regard as the worst thing of all: an implacable, insidious political foe. The nature of that foe goes by many names, and has become a shorthand for Western fears of violence and fanaticism, for all that is "uncivilised." As Leonard Lawlor notes: "In the simplest terms, the problem of the worst is apocalypse, complete suicide." The most visible sign of this problem, he avers, is the emergence of people "who kill themselves in order to kill others, leaving no one behind."[10] It is the suicide bomber, in short, who represents—according to the logic of both liberal and conservative mindsets—the "worst of the worst," the figure responsible for the most egregious worst-case scenario.[11]

But in the political dynamic that has taken shape since September 11, 2001, the terrorist does not, as it were, stand alone. His counterpart, on the other side of power, is the refugee. In the 1980s and 1990s, parts of Africa and the Balkans witnessed the phenomenon of "refugee camp militarisation," in which disaffected refugees were recruited by local militias; more recently, the military response to terrorism has brought about large-scale upheavals of civilian populations, which in turn has created significant numbers of homeless or otherwise destitute people.[12] Hence, there is a complementary bond that forces us to think together "terrorist" and "refugee," that brings them into close, congruous alignment, in the politics of the new millennium. From this angle, then, the refugee is also part of the problem of the worst.

To return now to *The Road*, the same problem is also apparent, albeit in a quite different, counter-Leibnizian guise. Upending the German philosopher's claim, in his *Essays on Theodicy* (1710), that, for all its flaws, this is the best of all possible worlds ("[I]t still remains true . . . that there is an infinitude of possible worlds among which God must needs have chosen the best"[13]), McCarthy envisages something of what the worst might be like. As his man and boy undertake their perilous journey to the Gulf Coast across what appears to be the Southeastern United States, they encounter violence, horror, and extreme hardship at every turn. The sun barely shines through permanent cloud-cover, a "rain of drifting soot" (14) envelops everything, and plants and animals are all but extinct. The scorched land and blackened trees suggest nuclear holocaust—*mementi mori* of a time when "[e]verything was on fire" (204)—and the atmospheric disturbances are symptomatic of nuclear winter (though none of the accompanying side effects, such as radiation sickness, is apparent).

It is not only the natural world and its seasonal variations that are in abeyance; language, too, has begun to erode, as any meaning beyond the immediate maintenance of life is leached from human deeds. The man recognizes the loss:

> He'd had this feeling before, beyond the numbness and the dull despair. The world shrinking down about a raw core of parsible entities. The names of things slowly following those things into oblivion. . . . The sacred idiom shorn of its referents and so of its reality. (93)

As if testing the veracity of this hypothesis, around the book's halfway mark a traveller on the road sounds them out. "What are you?" he asks them. To which the narrator reports: "They'd no way to answer the question." (172) The protagonists may not be able to answer, but know what they are, because they have already admitted to it in an earlier scene. The sight of woodsmoke on the horizon has the two wondering what manner of people might be camped-up there.

What should we do papa?
I think we should take a look. We just have to be careful. If it's a
commune they'll have barricades. But it may just be refugees.
Like us.
Yes. Like us. (82)

The man, the boy, and everyone else in *The Road* are refugees, seeking
asylum from the earth itself, vainly pitting themselves against the
dead shell that is the depleted biosphere. The book thus presents the
state of displaced homelessness as a national (and, we can impute, a
global) condition. But if being a refugee is the default status of every
human being in *The Road*, what then is the "worst"?

In the world McCarthy describes, every human being is forced
to become a scavenger, or die, to seize whatever he or she can of
the world's remaining resources—food, weapons, clothing, bodies.
At the far end of the scale is a more ill-defined species of scavenger:
the cannibal, for whom survival has become a monstrous, macabre
end in itself. As a practice, it connotes barbaric excess, (barely)
fathomable in the context of foreign custom or rite, but intolerable
in the context of Western social norms. McCarthy, then, plots a line
from the refugee to the cannibal, from scavenging to savagery—a
point of no return, the problem of the worst, made even worse.

It has become a truism to note, in the popular-cultural imaginary,
a resurgence of those two perennial envoys of the un-human,
zombies and vampires. But although both practice anthropophagy,
they elicit very different registers of feeling. Zombies are agents
of pure horror, inspiring revulsion and abhorrence; vampires,
conversely, possess an aura of aristocratic elegance and sexual
charisma, by turns attractive and repellent. Yet both creatures'
gothic-mythological allure puts them at a distance from cannibals,
who are all-too-human, as ethnographic studies have shown.
Or rather, cannibals belong to nature, rather than (or as well as)
mythology, which may account for the abiding fascination shown
by colonial studies scholars.[14] One of the more unpleasant ironies
of *The Road*, then, is that as nature recedes toward extinction, one
of its most rebarbative spawn undergoes a corresponding increase.

McCarthy's cannibals are more zombie than vampire: which is to
say, they are figures of abject horror, the point of absolute difference
(in the boy's scrupulous moral scale) between the "good guys" and
the "bad guys." Cannibals in *The Road* also part company with

vampires in a more figurative sense. It was Marx who first saw similarities between vampiric hunger and capitalist rapacity. "Capital is dead labour," he writes, "which, vampire-like, lives only by sucking living labour, and lives the more, the more labour it sucks."[15] The cannibal, by contrast, is the anti-capitalist par excellence. Instead of limitless accumulation, the cannibal survives by devouring his own kind, a figure of pure, non-replenishable consumption; Richard Pech and Geoffrey Durden summarize this as a turn away from the socially mindful inclination "to facilitate prosperity and growth" toward short-term, individual "self-aggrandizement."[16] The loss of civilization, therefore, is signified by a disconcerting compact: the absence of capitalist exploitation, in favor of the horrors and abominations of cannibal consumption.

Mapping "post-America"

Civilization is, of course, defined by more than just human conduct. Its most pervasive *physical* reminder in *The Road* is the road itself, the "black lines" on the map that denote the interstate routes. The road's significance is heightened by the fact that it is a metonymy, twice removed, of capitalist modernity—first, via America's once-mighty automotive industry, which necessitated the widespread construction of interstate freeways; and then through the Fordist methods of mass-production which made that industry thrive, between the 1940s and the 1960s. As the only remaining marker of what was once an auspicious industrial civilization, the road convokes a strangely ominous and suspenseful space, suggestive of a threatening, uncanny "post-America."[17] But the road, which ensures direct passage through the blasted terrain, is also tied in direct ways with human behavior. The man and the boy's journey is permanently fraught with danger because the road entails *visibility*, and this, in turn, convokes *vulnerability*, that is, exposure to others. In the man's reworked system of values, in the new hunter-scavenger economy, potentially the worst thing of all is others, because others, as a general rule, mean death.

There is a psychoanalytic dimension to this alignment of others with violence and death. In "Aggressivity in Psychoanalysis" (1949), Jacques Lacan portrays the other as a recognizable and analogous entity, in pursuit of the same objects in the world as the self. The "aggressivity" that ensues—Lacan defines it as "a correlative tension of the narcissistic structure in the coming-into-being of the subject"—thus has ontological underpinnings, which suggests that rivalry is inevitable, and explains "the pre-eminence of aggressivity in our civilization."[18] However, Lacan routes aggressivity through "paranoic knowledge" (17), the erotic relation (19) and the Oedipal complex (22–4), creating a somewhat more byzantine scenario than the stark, almost elegantly minimalist situation depicted in *The Road*. I suggest then, that a more appropriate model for McCarthy's pared-down, post-cultural America is Hegel's equally primal account of intersubjective encounter in the lordship-bondsman section of the *Phenomenology*.[19]

In Hegel's exposition, when one burgeoning self-consciousness meets another, a struggle to the death ensues. The one willing to go all the way, and risk annihilation, becomes the master, or lord, and the other, unwilling or unable to take that risk, becomes the slave, or bondsman.[20] So, too, in *The Road* is this kind of violent struggle more than just a daily possibility; in the limited contact the man and the boy have with other human beings, it becomes almost a given. However, as with the Leibnizian example, McCarthy turns Hegel on his head. Instead of a necessary stage in the development of social being, violent rivalry connotes *regression*, as the remnants of the human race withhold recognition and move in the opposite direction, becoming more asocial, atomized, and self-interested. This regressive tendency also brings to light a particularly prominent antecedent, in a work laden with intertextual allusions.

It was once *de rigueur* to cite Faulkner and Melville (McCarthy's favorite authors) as models for his late-modernist project. *The Road* breaks with this tendency, prompting comparisons with Twain,[21] with Hemingway,[22] with Steinbeck,[23] and, interestingly, with Flannery O'Connor.[24] But an equally insistent "ghost" in the text, that has thus far eluded proper critical explication, is Samuel Beckett.[25] *Fin de Partie*, or *Endgame* (1956), is the paradigmatic work, an end-of-the-world scenario that takes place in permanent grey light, in the wake of an unnamed catastrophe, and that explores the dynamic of the father-son relationship (albeit in more malicious ways). Beckett's singular example, however—his dislocating "lessness"—is most pronounced in several of the characters that the man and boy encounter.

McCarthy's post-America is peopled by vagrants who seem to have strayed from the pages of Beckett's fiction—loners who are committed, insofar as they show any commitment at all, to their own dereliction. (The "Beckett man," writes Anthony Cronin, "is a lone individual who regards others with fear, hatred, impatience or contempt."[26]) The first of these, nicknamed the "burned man" because he has been struck by lightning, is an apparition-like figure who seems to personify the blasted land, "as burntlooking as the country, his clothing scorched and black . . . a nitty wig of ash upon his blackened skull" (51); he appears and disappears without real contact (51). And the third one, a thief who relieves them of their entire belongings, is little more than a generic tramp, "[s]crawny, sullen, bearded, filthy" (273). It is the second figure, the "traveller," that is closest to the Beckettian archetype, though taken to one extreme: "An old man, small and bent" who "looked like a pile of rags fallen off a cart" (171–2). The traveller calls himself "Ely," a kind of reincarnation of Melville's "Elijah" from *Moby-Dick* ("a stranger . . . shabbily apparelled in faded jacket and patched trowsers; a rag of a black handkerchief investing his neck"[27]). Yet when the Man asks him if wishes he had never been born, the traveller's response could have been scripted by Beckett: "Well. Beggars cant be choosers. . . . What's done is done. Anyway, it's foolish to ask for luxuries in times like these." (180)

McCarthy then crosses Beckett with Melville, invoking an audacious biblical allusion. In a work where proper names are non-existent, "Ely" admits that this is not his real name—"I don't want anybody talking about me. . . . I could be anybody" [182]—and closes the gap between Melville's stranger and the prophet Elijah, who lived 800 years before Christ. He appears in the Bible in the first book of Kings, warning of a catastrophic drought that will ravage the land of Israel. Like Melville's stranger, Ely, too, claims his own powers of divination: "I knew this was coming. . . . This or something like it. I always believed in it." (179) The scene has received its share of negative critical responses; Steve Gehrke, for example, sees it as a half-hearted attempt at concretizing the religious insinuations, and deems it the "least successful [scene] in the novel."[28] Yet Ely's "prophecy" reiterates the precarious relationship between civilization and nature, upon which lies the book's premise. Further, the appearance of the decrepit old vagrant compels the man to think an odd thought about the boy: "Perhaps he'd turn into a god and they to trees." (173) This is a telling moment, juxtaposing the supernatural with the natural, and setting the man's messianic hopes alongside one of the fundamental components of "bare life," namely, the metamorphic lure of arboreal structures.

The emergence of alter-nature

I suggested earlier that *The Road* ought not to be seen as engaging in any meaningful way with ruminations about climate change. Nevertheless, the book can still be read—without irony, I hasten to add—as an extended nature poem. Plaintive, rather than exultant, the work elegizes nature, providing evidence every few pages of its abiding significance. Having first been made strange by the unrepresentable Event, nature continues to assert itself through the climatic indicators of ashen air and fire-ravaged land, purging the world of the bucolic charms of the pastoral and putting the focus instead on the terrors and consternations of the sublime. The book's most formidable imaginative feat, then, is to bring into being this alter-nature, whose deregulated processes make the natural realm more tomb than haven.

If McCarthy uses the road to invoke American capitalism, his synecdoche for nature is trees. They feature in almost every section of the book, past and present, assuming manifold guises. As bearers of fruit, and hence indicative of life, trees are predicates of survival. The only respite the protagonists have from their enforced diet of canned, preserved or dried goods comes when the man discovers, against all the odds, an apple in some dead grass. Hard, shriveled, and almost tasteless, it is a bitter retort to the ur-apple, the fruit of knowledge that gets Adam and Eve cast out of Eden. But this anti-Eden connotes more than just another "lost paradise," because it links *The Road* to McCarthy's earliest work. His first novels return again and again to the loss of the American myth of virtue and innocence—a myth derived from the "Puritan vision of a sanctified national mission in an Edenic paradise."[29] Seen through this lens, the moldering apple and decaying orchard signify the final erasure of America's national mythology, that finds its epicenter at the nature-culture nexus. Nature, then, is first linked to civilization, and then used to show its decline.

The counterpart to this scene is the man's vivid childhood reverie, in which he recalls dragging a tree-stump across the water in his uncle's rowboat. The pathos of the memory turns, once again, on the unbridgeable gulf between the lost past, with its surplus of nature, in which trees deposited in a lake have no effect on forestation, and the barren present, in which nature's death-throes are the only indication of its former potency. Yet even as the withered leftovers of an almost-extinct natural order, trees are still endemic to human survival. They provide an almost unlimited supply of fuel—the fires having reduced the forests to so much dead wood—when winter sets in.

In addition to trees as once-living sources of food, and as now-inert stores of fuel, trees in the novel are wont to fall. And when they do, *The Road* becomes, once again, a philosophical fable. George Berkeley's doctrine of "subjective idealism" posits that to be is to be perceived (*esse est percipi*), that perception underwrites being. He writes: "The objects of sense exist only when they are no longer perceived; the trees therefore are in the garden . . . no longer than while there is somebody there to perceive them."[30] Loosely derived from this credo is the popular conundrum, "If a tree falls in a forest and no one is around to hear it, does it make a sound?" The sound of falling trees in *The Road* cannot provide any ontological guarantees because God, Berkeley's "author of nature," is not present to hear them. These falling trees are, in fact, forecasts of future absence—as nature recedes into memory, and memory is slowly but surely extinguished. So even as falling trees in McCarthy's novel have the unalloyed austerity of a Berkeleyan thought-experiment, they are as double-sided as everything in the novel associated with civilization. The trees that keep the protagonists alive, or at least prevent them from freezing to death, are also the trees that signify the demise of nature.

McCarthy's exploitation of tree imagery, and its associations, takes place within a wider historical web of allusion. In keeping with this, I want to consider now two very different examples of "tree theory," as a way of illustrating the diminished reach of McCarthy's alter-nature. In the first instance, let us look to Deleuze and Guattari, and their acerbic remarks in *A Thousand Plateaus*. What they call "state philosophy"—rigid, monolithic, authoritarian—is, for them, a kind of "worst." Extrapolating from this, the arborescent model of thinking that such philosophy spawns could be seen as the "worst of the worst." "We're tired of trees," they write. "We should stop believing in trees, roots, and radicles. They've made us suffer too much. All of arborescent culture is founded on them, from biology to linguistics."[31] The tree or root, they say, is a centralizing conductor for power and hierarchy that "plots a point, fixes an order" (7); hence their resistance to "tree logic," which arises because this model "has dominated Western reality and all of Western thought" (18). It has done so through metaphors used to describe the organization of human knowledge, in which all is fixity, unity, totality. The tree model, in other words, resists *becoming*; it does not permit the dispersion and propagation that Deleuze and Guattari find in the rhizome.

Coming from an entirely different direction, Franco Moretti avows, by way of contrast, that the tree model *does* enable a certain amount of difference—or, to use his term, "morphological novelty" (90). Where Deleuze and Guattari's focus is on monolithic "trunk-forms," Moretti, in *Graphs, Maps, Trees*, emphasizes "branch-forms," the ways in which tree-limbs split off and interconnect. In his estimate, the so-called "morphological tree" is defined by the "incessant growing-apart of life forms."[32] Both organic evolution and cultural development adhere to the same cyclical pattern of *divergence* and *convergence*, or branching-out followed by syncretism, followed by further branching-out, etc. If it is not as open-ended as rhizomatic dissemination, neither is it bound to the rigid, linear schemas imposed by "tree logic."

What is most striking about the post cultural landscape of *The Road* is that it repudiates *both* models. McCarthy shows just how unstable "trunk-forms" are—fragile, provisional, not at all the monolithic purveyors of power and authority that Deleuze and Guattari describe. Everything is unfixed, in the worst of all possible worlds, but this unfixity does not allow for divergence, not even in Moretti's restricted sense. Trees thus connote not only the lost past and the shattered present, but also the fatally diminished future. (Similarly, although the road itself is what Deleuze and Guattari would call "nomad space"—a smooth, open-ended space of potential—it is, as we have seen, contaminated by Hegelian violence, its transformative openness used to stage deadly struggles for mastery.) Is there any possibility for deliverance or recovery, in this scenario of enveloping desolation? "All the trees in the world are going to fall sooner or later," says the man. "But not on us" (35)—as if they will somehow escape the depredations of biospheric collapse. The tone of this remark, pitched somewhere between fatalism and hope, encapsulates the covert religious passion that is the crux of the present enquiry.

The road already taken

To assay *The Road*'s religious orientation, let us turn once again to the question of the "worst." In the early 1980s, Samuel Beckett undertook a comprehensive analysis of the question in a dense, elegiac novella entitled *Worstward Ho* (1983). His last sustained reflection on the afflictions of being, Alain Badiou calls it a "testamental text," a work that attempts to "take stock of the whole of Samuel Beckett's intellectual enterprise."[33] James Knowlson, Beckett's biographer, locates the origin of this "poetics of worstness" in some lines from *King Lear*, when Edgar struggles to find meaning amidst barbarism ("The lamentable change is from the best, / The worst returns to laughter"[34]). However, I want to propose a more recent source, from a writer who elsewhere exerted a powerful influence on Beckett. In "The Second Coming" (1920), W. B. Yeats offers a formulation that addresses the ironic perplexity and disquiet of the modern age: "The best lack all conviction, while the worst / Are full of passionate intensity."[35] The chiasmic structure of this formulation unsettles any assumptions about hierarchy or priority; in the poem's apocalyptic schema, such tidy distinctions are as contestable as all the other Western traditions fated to undergo a Nietzschean "revaluation of all values."[36]

Beckett takes Yeats's chiasmic formulation and condenses it, reworking the matters that occupied him throughout his writing life—indigence, failure, exhaustion, decrepitude—into the encompassing term, "worstness." To be more precise, he elaborates the poem's implicit revaluation by exploring every permutation of "best" and "worst," effectively constructing a whole idiom out of their confluence. This runs the gamut from the "less worse" to the "better worse," the "best worse," and the "worst in need of worse."[37] If "worstness" is our fate, as Beckett suggests—and if we cannot fend off or mitigate it—then the only way forward is by means of the verb "to worsen," that is, to acknowledge it as a condition, rather than treat it as a fallacy or misapprehension. McCarthy all but adverts to a similar state of affairs in present-day America, in the guise of religious fundamentalism.

On the side of "civilization," as we have seen, lies (the debris of) American capitalism, whose best-and-worst qualities are embodied in the road itself—an industrial feat refigured into an arena of violence. Thus, the unnamed catastrophe has not wiped out an unspoilt way of life, but revealed the outlines of its contradictions. This is complicated still further when we factor in, as gauges of civilization, the tormented voice of religious hope (the man) and the uncorrupted voice of moral conscience (the boy). The latter's instincts are to share, to assist, to take care of others—instincts that are otherwise absent from the world, and that are at odds with the man's more cynical, pragmatic attitude. Because of this tension, the boy occasionally needs reassuring that they are the "good guys," that they belong to the "best" rather than the "worst." This reassurance takes the form of a somewhat enigmatic avowal, repeated like a mantra:

> We're going to be okay, arent we Papa?
> Yes. We are.
> And nothing bad it going to happen to us.
> That's right.
> Because we're carrying the fire.
> Yes. Because we're carrying the fire.

Though it is never fully explained what it means to "carry the fire," it suggests the original Christian meaning of the word "immanence": the divine presence whose flame burns *within*, as opposed to God's transcendence *without*, beyond or outside of creation. This interpretation is given credence by the man's belief that the boy is, in some sense, the Chosen One—the promise that will deliver them from the privation and dread that have become everyday life. The claim that they are "carrying the fire" is literalized toward the end, when the boy keeps watch over the dying man ("The light was a candle which the boy bore in a ringstick of beaten copper" [299–300]). Yet fire is also the instrument of global catastrophe, the medium that has devastated the land, generating ash ("ashes to ashes") that has blotted out the sun and polluted the air. The "best" and the "worst" are thus embodied in an element with unequivocal religious connotations.

These connotations also invoke the "civilising" mission of Christian evangelism, which reaches back several centuries, but it is a more recent phenomenon in American religious culture. As Ralph W. Hood, Jr. et al. note, "[T]hrough most of the nineteenth century . . . American civilisation and [Bible-based] Protestantism were mutually supportive, if not synonymous."[38] That association continues into the early twentieth century, with the birth of American (Protestant) fundamentalism,[39] whose code of belief evinces a curious mixture of incompatible attitudes. On the one hand, it insists on the divinity of Christ, and freely invokes his name whenever the rhetoric of salvation and personal redemption is exercised ("What would Jesus have done?"). But at the same time, the disposition underpinning this rhetoric is far from the appeal to charity, forgiveness, and neighborly love that suffuses the New Testament. Indeed, it more closely resembles that of the wrathful, punitive God of the Old Testament, in its pre-Christian fixation on sin and transgression (tellingly, fundamentalist reprovals are almost always couched in allusions to Old Testament pedagogy).

The man's temperament mirrors this two-sided fundamentalist view. In the first instance, he treats his son with almost limitless love, care, and protection. Put simply, this suggests that the boy functions for the man as an instrument of meaning, a vehicle whereby value can be restored to the world. The man's method, then, is not unlike a Rortian "redescription": he takes the framework of nineteenth-century eschatology, which sees civilization in decline and anticipates the return of a redeemer, and reads it into the grim, vanishing present. But the man also fosters an intransigent fundamentalism, voiced when he says to the boy: "My job is to take care of you. I was appointed to do that by God. I will kill anyone who touches you." (80) Even more revealing is the scene of retribution, when the protagonists catch up with the thief. As the boy pleads with the man to spare his life, the thief is forced to surrender not only the stolen belongings, but his own "vile rags" and shoes as well. "I'm going to leave you the way you left us" (276), the man tells him; an eye for an eye, in other words, which amounts to a slow death warrant for the thief.

Given these implied fundamentalist correspondences, to what extent can McCarthy be said to address Rorty's exhortation for a "postreligious" American culture? Religious fundamentalism is, of course, central to the "problem of the worst"—suicide bombing as the most heinous form of Islamic violence against the West. But rather than denouncing or demonizing, McCarthy relocates the problem to home soil. The most sinister "ghost" in *The Road*, then, is the Western response to the "worstness" of Islam—a response informed by the Christian fundamentalist attitude outlined above, and given explicit voice by George Bush on September 16, 2001 ("This *crusade*, this war on terrorism, is going to take a while").[40] The Bush administration's ensuing interventions thus constitute a thinly veiled "holy war," staged to bring democracy to the oppressed heathens, but in the process revealing itself as contradictory, confused, and deeply troubling.

The confounding of distinctions between "best" and "worst" is reiterated by Ely, the traveller, whose namesake Elijah means "my God is Jehovah" (or Yahweh). Ely both affirms and denies his namesake. "There is no God," he tells the man, "and we are his prophets" (181) (A similarly aporetic expostulation occurs in *Endgame*, when Hamm says of the deity: "The bastard! He doesn't exist!" [38]). When Ely first meets the protagonists, he says "I've not seen a fire in a long time" (183), and takes the boy for some kind of celestial vision. "What if I said he's a god?" the man tentatively suggests. Ely's response ("I'm past all that now") identifies him as a prophet of nihilism:

> Where men cant live gods fare no better. You'll see. It's better to be alone. So I hope that's not true what you said because to be on the road with the last god would be a terrible thing so I hope it's not true. Things will be better when everybody's gone. . . . When we're all gone at least then there'll be nobody here but death and his days will be numbered too. (183–4)

This is the "Beckett man" at his most uncompromising—clinging fiercely to solitude and looking forward to oblivion, and, implied erudition notwithstanding, seeing civilization as a needless encumbrance. But Ely's speech also warrants a comparison with McCarthy's earlier and more sustaining master, William Faulkner. In *As I Lay Dying*, the Bundren's disenchanted doctor, Peabody, says:

> I can remember how when I was young I believed death to be a phenomenon of the body; now I know it to be merely a function of the mind – and that of the minds of the ones who suffer bereavement. The nihilists say it is the end; the fundamentalists,

the beginning; when in reality it is no more than a single tenant or family moving out of a tenement or a town.[41]

Fundamentalism or nihilism: McCarthy does not quite come to say, like Faulkner's Peabody, that they are all of a piece, and that death is just a "function of the mind," a way of seeing the world. The two outlooks—and their increasingly indistinct analogues, civilization and barbarism—would seem to be the only choices on offer, in the post-political, post-religious America of *The Road*. But McCarthy's bleak prognosis is not based on any misguided belief in the power of reform. The road worstward is not something to be either chosen or avoided, in the politico-religious landscape that defines the new millennium. Rather, it is the road we have already taken.

Notes

1 Richard Rorty, *Contingency, Irony, and Solidarity* (Cambridge: Cambridge University Press, 1989), p. xvi.

2 Robert Elder, "Never-Ending Fire," rev. of *The Road, Touchstone* (April 2008): 34–5.

3 Lee Brewer Jones, "Prophet of Hope?" rev. of *The Road, The Chattahoochie Review* (Fall 2006): 182.

4 Carl James Grindley, "The Setting of McCarthy's *The Road*," *The Explicator* 67.1 (2008): 11

5 Thomas H. Schaub, "Secular Scripture and Cormac McCarthy's *The Road*," *Renascence: Essays on Value in Literature* 61.3 (Spring 2009): 156.

6 Thomas A. Carlson, "With the World at Heart: Reading Cormac McCarthy's *The Road* with Augustine and Heidegger," *Religion and Literature* 39.3 (2007): 57.

7 George Monbiot, "Civilisation ends with a shutdown of human concern. Are we there already?" *The Guardian* (30 October 2007).

8 Giorgio Agamben, *Homo Sacer: Sovereign Power and Bare Life*, trans. Daniel Heller-Roazen (Stanford: Stanford University Press, 1998), p. 8.

9 Richard Gray, "Open Doors, Closed Minds: American prose writing at a time of crisis," *American Literary History* 21.1 (2009): 139.

10 Leonard Lawlor, "'There Will Never Be Enough Done': An Essay on the Problem of the Worst in Deleuze and Guattari," *Divination* 28 (Autumn–Winter 2008): 119.

11 The term "worst of the worst" was coined by the then Secretary of
    Defense, Donald Rumsfeld, in 2002. Guantánamo Bay, he announced,
    was to be used as a holding-pen for containing "the worst of the
    worst," dangerous prisoners from the war on terror intent on
    harming innocent civilians. George W. Bush later used the same
    expression to dampen any sympathy for the Bay's inmates, when
    human rights abuses started to come to light. See Katherine Q. Seelye,
    "Threats and Responses: The Detainees," *The New York Times* (23
    October 2002): A14.

12 Robert Muggah, "Once we were warriors: critical reflections on
    refugee and IDP militarisation and human security," in *Human
    Security and Non-Citizens: Law, Policy and International Affairs,* ed.
    A. Edwards, C. Ferstman (Cambridge: Cambridge University Press
    2010), 170–3.

13 G. W. Leibniz, *Theodicy: Essays on the Goodness of God and the
    Freedom of Man and the Origin of Evil,* trans. E. M. Huggard
    (London: Routledge & Kegan Paul 1951), p. 128.

14 Peter Hulme, "Introduction: The Cannibal Scene," in *Cannibalism
    and the Colonial World,* ed. F. Barker, P. Hulme, M. Iversen
    (Cambridge: Cambridge University Press 1998), pp. 3–6.

15 Karl Marx, *Capital Vol. One,* trans. Ben Fowkes (Harmondsworth:
    Penguin 1990), p. 342.

16 Richard J. Pech and Geoffrey Durden, "Where the Decision-Makers
    went Wrong: from Capitalism to Cannibalism," *Corporate Governance:
    International Journal of Business in Society* 4.1 (2004): 68.

17 More troubling, it seems to me, is the scene in which the man
    discovers an unopened can of Coca-Cola, and bids the boy to drink
    it. Shorn of its iconic, mediatized aura, the drink conveys for the boy
    a sweet, bubbly treat, and nothing more; the affectless quality of the
    scene turns the object into a poignant reminder of a lost civilization.
    Yet at the same time, it is disquieting, for precisely the opposite
    reason: the suggestion that this product can survive not only the loss
    of its co-referent (Coke = America), but also the end of the world,
    with its flavor intact.

18 Jacques Lacan, *Écrits: A Selection,* trans. Alan Sheridan (New York
    and London: W.W. Norton & Co., 1977), pp. 22, 25.

19 Lacan is himself deferential in this regard: "[Hegel] provided the
    ultimate theory of the proper function of aggressivity in human
    ontology, seeming to prophecy the iron law of our time. From the
    conflict of Master and Slave, he deduced the entire subjective and
    objective progress of our history," *Écrits,* p. 26.

20 G. W. F. Hegel, *Phenomenology of Spirit,* trans. A. V. Miller (Oxford:
    Oxford University Press, 1977), pp. 111–18.

21 Jones, "Prophet of Hope?", p. 184.

22 Steve Gehrke, rev. of *The Road*, *The Missouri Review* 30.1 (2007): 152; Schaub, "Secular Scripture," 156–7.

23 Linda Woodson, "Mapping *The Road* in Post-Postmodernism," *The Cormac McCarthy Journal* 6 (Autumn 2008): 88.

24 Schaub, "Secular Scripture," 158.

25 James Wood, for example, compares (unfavorably) McCarthy's "reticence" and "minimalism" to Beckett's; Euan Gallivan makes a brief reference to Beckett's *Watt*, in the context of Schopenhauerian ethics; see Gallivan, "Compassionate McCarthy?: *The Road* and Schopenhauerian Ethics," *The Cormac McCarthy Journal* 6, (Autumn 2008): 104; and Richard Gray hears the closing words of *The Unnamable* ("you must go on, I can't go on, I'll go on") echoed in the refusal of McCarthy's protagonists to accept annihilation, "Open Doors, Closed Minds," 139.

26 Anthony Cronin, *Samuel Beckett: The Last Modernist* (London: Flamingo, 1997), p. 379.

27 Herman Melville, *Moby-Dick; or, The Whale* (Harmondsworth: Penguin, 1986), p. 188.

28 Gehrke, rev. of *The Road*, p. 151.

29 Vince Brewton, "The Changing Landscape of Violence in Cormac McCarthy's Early Novels and the Border Trilogy," *Southern Literary Journal* 37.1 (Fall 2004): 124.

30 George Berkeley, *A Treatise Concerning the Principles of Human Knowledge* (Oxford and New York: Oxford University Press, 1998), par. 45.

31 Gilles Deleuze and Guattari, Félix *A Thousand Plateaus*, trans. Brian Massumi (Minneapolis and London: University of Minnesota Press, 1987), p. 15.

32 Franco Moretti, *Graphs, Maps, Trees: Abstract Models for a Literary History* (London: Verso, 2005), p. 70.

33 Alain Badiou, "Being, Existence, Thought: Prose and Concept" in *On Beckett: Essays and Criticism*, ed. N. Power, A. Toscano (Manchester: Clinamen Press, 2003), p. 80.

34 James Knowlson, *Damned to Fame: The Life of Samuel Beckett* (London: Bloomsbury, 1996), p. 674.

35 W. B. Yeats, *The Poems*, ed. D. Albright (London: Everyman, 1992), p. 235.

36 As has been noted, the father's dream in the opening scene of *The Road* invokes Yeats's final image of unholy terror, the "rough beast" that "Slouches towards Bethlehem" (see Schaub, "Secular Scripture," p. 154; Grindley, "The Setting of McCarthy's *The Road*," p. 12).

37 Samuel Beckett, *Nohow On* (London: John Calder, 1989), p. 117.

38 Ralph W. Hood, Jr., Peter C. Hill, and W. Paul Williamson, *The Psychology of American Fundamentalism* (New York and London: Guildford Press, 2005), p. 50.

39 "Fundamentalism," as a term pertaining to American Protestantism, was coined in 1920, to denote "militant conservatives in the Northern Baptist Convention" (Hood, Jr., et al., *Psychology of American Fundamentalism*, p. 48).

40 George W. Bush, "Remarks by the President Upon Arrival," Office of the Press Secretary, 2001; emphasis added. Online (accessed 2 November 2011): http://georgewbush-whitehouse.archives.gov/news/releases/2001/09/20010916-2.html

41 William Faulkner, *As I Lay Dying* (New York: Vintage, 1985), pp. 43–4.

7

The cave and *The Road*: Styles of forgotten dreams

JULIAN MURPHET

The animal, the sacred

The opening image of Cormac McCarthy's *The Road* is a dream-image of a cave. In it, we are given to behold the Beast of the Apocalypse itself, bleached to translucence by centuries of stony sleep:

> In the dream from which he'd wakened he had wandered in a cave where the child led him by the hand. . . . Until they stood in a great stone room where lay a black and ancient lake. And on the far shore a creature that raised its dripping mouth from the rimstone pool and stared into the light with dead eyes white and sightless as the eggs of spiders. It swung its head low over the water as if to take the scent of what it could not see. Crouching there pale and naked and translucent, its alabaster bones cast up in shadow on the rocks behind it. Its bowels, its beating heart. The brain that pulsed in a dull glass bell. It swung its head from side to side and then gave out a low moan and turned and lurched away and loped soundlessly into the dark. (1–2)

This, one of several animal visions in the novel, resonates powerfully with the strange closing minutes of Werner Herzog's *Cave of*

Forgotten Dreams (2011). In a "Postscript" to his three-dimensional
journey into Chauvet Cave, Herzog muses on the post-historical
anomaly of a nearby greenhouse, heated by the runoff waters of a
nuclear power plant, where mutant albino crocodiles crouch in the
tropical warmth, and stare back from an imaginable greenhouse-
gas futurity at a moribund cinema-going humanity, as transient in
turn as the decorators of Chauvet. Like McCarthy's, this image is a
"vision," a fever dream not mortgaged to any empirical facts, but
engendered by what Herzog calls "ecstatic truth."[1] In both visions,
a style of dreaming is assayed in which the pre-historical and the
post-historical overlap; in which an "alabaster" animal blindly
returns the gaze of a human being who cannot internalize its truth.

Herzog's film concerns the inauguration of a properly human
spirit. Reconstructing that spirit out of the evidence left printed on
the walls of Chauvet, *The Cave of Forgotten Dreams* postulates
(in keeping with an established line of thinking) that it was at the
moment when hominids gave symbolic-mimetic shape to their animal
cohort, that a spiritual hole was bored into the tight-knit weave of
natural phenomena. Into that bottomless hole, to conjure away the
fear of animal threat, these hominids cast names; in the chant made
by those names, in fire-lit dances before the animal shapes imprinted
on the walls, "man" was born, and with him the gods. "The gasp of
surprise which accompanies the experience of the unusual becomes
its name. It fixes the transcendence of the unknown in relation to
the known, and therefore terror as sacredness."[2] Giorgio Agamben,
in his essay *The Open: Man and Animal*, muses: "Even the most
luminous sphere of our relations with the divine depends, in some
way, on that darker one which separates us from the animal."[3] It is
a plausible account, made almost irrefutable by the traces left upon
the mineral depths of Chauvet: the simultaneous birth of humanity
and divinity, in the act of rendering animals in symbolic form.

In the literary tradition of the United States, no one feature so
characterizes what McCarthy calls its "sacred idiom" (93) as the
effort to do justice to its native fauna—to forge a style and a rhythm
out of the English language, ridding it of its trans-Atlantic debt to
skylarks and cuckoos and English deer, and attuning it to life-forms
orphaned of names by the extermination of the First Nations. To
be sure, no effort, however noble, could ever hope to overcome
that catastrophic holocaust of "world" in Heidegger's sense: the
ruination of those fecund matrices of sky, earth, mortals and divinity
(the "fourfold"), held in place by names, in which "the things named

are called into their thinging. Thinging, they unfold world."[4] Given
the violent unstringing of such sacred worlds—be they Iroquois or
Algonquian or Sioux—by European powers, no attempt to fashion
a new one could ever redeem the blood debt. Yet, after Emerson's
injunctions, there is a tremendous vitality in the attempt. From his
own "screaming of the wild geese flying by night; the thin note of
the companionable titmouse, in the winter day; the fall of swarms
of flies, in autumn, from combats high in the air, pattering down on
the leaves like rain"[5]; through Thoreau's pickerel:

> They possess a quite dazzling and transcendent beauty which
> separates them by a wide interval from the cadaverous cod
> and haddock whose fame is trumpeted in our streets. They are
> not green like the pines, nor gray like the stones, nor blue like
> the sky; but they have, to my eyes, if possible, yet rarer colors,
> like flowers and precious stones, as if they were the pearls, the
> animalized *nuclei* or crystals of the Walden water[6]

to Whitman's teeming itinerary of pond life:

> the tremulous, reedy call of some bird from recesses, breaking
> the warm, indolent, half-voluptuous silence; an occasional wasp,
> hornet, honey-bee or bumble (they hover near my hands or face,
> yet annoy me not, nor I them, as they appear to examine, find
> nothing, and away they go)—the vast space of the sky overhead
> so clear, and the buzzard up there sailing his slow whirl in
> majestic spirals and discs; just over the surface of the pond, two
> large slate-color'd dragon-flies, with wings of lace, circling and
> darting and occasionally balancing themselves quite still, their
> wings quivering all the time[7]

the test of a post-native literature has been its ability to create a
"local habitation and a name" for the animal. Stylistically, what
works in such bodyings-forth is a specific coefficient of positivism
and unbridled parataxis, in which similes, conjunctive or disjunctive,
appear like gratuitous flourishes of languid spirit.

In the greatest American animal writing, in Melville's *Moby-
Dick*, Jack London's *White Fang* and *Call of the Wild*, Faulkner's
"The Bear," and some of Hemingway's work, the "sacred idiom"
is honed to an astonishing perfection—precisely in compensation
for what is already felt to be its imminent extinction. The most

unforgettable image of *Moby-Dick*, in which a vision of becalmed whale cows and calves emerges from within the churning horror of a bloody hunt, sets the tone for a century of paradoxical lamentation to come.[8] The worlds, and the gods, that this writing conjures up are already in the process of passing away, dying at the hands of the very mortal charged with hymning their names. "To be named," Walter Benjamin noted, "perhaps always brings with it a presentiment of mourning."[9] No body of writers ever seized this truth with the sincerity of these Americans. Faulkner's story is perhaps the quintessential installment in their multi-generational threnodic chant. The gods it calls forth—Old Ben, Lion, and their spiritual conductor, Sam Fathers—achieve immortality in the hunt that variously kills all of them, and that instantiates an inexorable social tendency to convert a spiritual commonwealth into the sacrilege of private property.[10]

In Hemingway's "Big Two-Hearted River," the brook trout have survived a devastation by fire of the entire township of Seney. Nick's first sighting of these creatures triggers an immeasurable affect of joy in his body; it is an affect made material by the fact that these may be the two longest sentences in the Hemingway canon:

> He watched them holding themselves with their noses into the current, many trout in deep, fast moving water, slightly distorted as he watched far down through the glassy convex surface of the pool, its surface pushing and swelling smooth against the resistance of the log-driven piles of the bridge. . . .
>
> As the shadow of the kingfisher moved up the stream, a big trout shot upstream in a long angle, only his shadow marking the angle, then lost his shadow as he came through the surface of the water, caught the sun, and then, as he went back into the stream under the surface, his shadow seemed to float down the stream with the current, unresisting, to his post under the bridge where he tightened facing up into the current.[11]

If Hemingway avoids all simile and metaphor, and commits himself to straight description, it is because in such flowing periods an unadorned nominalism is sublated into spirituality. The god of the river here appears, neither as an animal, nor as its concept, but as the breath and pulse of a language delivered over to the animal's being: its movement and rhythm as a "thinging" of world. That Nick then goes fishing in this holy place is simultaneously a rite of American manhood, and a sacking of the god's temple. The sacred that is attested to is immediately violated; the sacrificial animal is the node of that double vision, which is also a dialectical temporality—where ends and origins coincide.

Cormac McCarthy joins this tradition as its St John of Patmos. He takes the abiding crux of a modern American sacred idiom—the sacrificial animal, the living-dead god—and strips it to an incarnadine Revelation. The sacred idiom is reset in the key of apocalypse. Where Thoreau had heard, in the whine of a mosquito, nothing less than "something cosmical . . . a standing advertisement, till forbidden, of the everlasting vigor and fertility of the world,"[12] McCarthy makes a death-mask of this sanguine, Leibnizian view of intensive vitality.[13] Consider the image of extinction that appears in the later pages of *Blood Meridian, or the Evening Redness in the West.*

> It was an old hunter in camp and the hunter shared tobacco with him and told him of the buffalo and the stands he'd made against them, laid up in a sag on some rise with the dead animals scattered over the grounds and the herd beginning to mill and the riflebarrel so hot the wiping patches sizzled in the bore and the animals by the thousands and tens of thousands and the hides pegged out over actual square miles of ground . . . and the flint hides by the ton and hundred ton and the meat rotting on the ground and the air whining with flies and the buzzards and ravens and the night a horror of snarling and feeding with the wolves half crazed and wallowing in the carrion.[14]

This avatar of the Hemingway fisherman and the Faulkner bear-hunter continues: "On this ground alone between the Arkansas River and the Concho there was eight million carcasses. . . . We ransacked the country. Six weeks. Finally found a herd of eight animals and we killed them and come in. They're gone. Ever one of them that God ever made is gone as if they'd never been at all." (*BM*, 317) Or not quite, for this desertion leaves behind traces that do more than merely announce an absence: "the crazed and sunchalked bones of the vanished herds" (*BM*, 317) are an excessive remainder, marking the earth with a positive charge—the current of apocalypse. "The bones had been gathered into windrows ten feet high and hundreds long or into great conical hills topped with the signs or brands of their owners." (*BM*, 318) The "millennial herds" of buffalo have become mountainous cairns, transformed into portents of the End itself.

"I wonder," muses the old buffalo hunter, "if there's other worlds like this... Or if this is the only one." (*BM*, 317) In a similar vein, old Mr Johnson says in *Cities of the Plain*: "And it had always seemed to me that something can live and die but that the kind of thing that they were was always there. I didn't know you could poison that."[15] McCarthy's narratives know that you can, and that the poison is already pumping through the arterial system of Being. It is the poison of a creeping namelessness, of a silence so primeval as to be postmodern. "What is a country without rabbits and partridges?," asked Thoreau. "That must be a poor country indeed that does not support a hare."[16] A world is impoverished disproportionately by such lack, bled dry of its "salitter."[17] The "yammer and yap of the . . . wolves" (*BM*, 318) is what old man Johnson misses: "I ain't heard a wolf howl in thirty odd years. I don't know where you'd go to hear one. There may not be any such a place." (*BT*, 870) This is what it is like to lose a world, to feel it come apart around you, in the absence of animal speech.[18] It is the coda to the story in *The Crossing*, of the last local wolf alive, led by the boy Billy Parham back into the supposed safety of the mountains south of the Mexican border, only to meet an absolute doom. Appropriated by a gang of horsemen to be used for entertainment before a wealthy *hacendado*, the hapless *lupus* is chained to a stake and baited by teams of fighting Airedales; until, pushed from animal instinct into pure drive, the wolf ends up a "sorry thing to see," a fitting spectacle of species exhaustion, and is mercy-killed (*BT*, 430). But in a final sacrament, Billy composes a praise-giving song for this wolf in the dying moments of his boyhood:

> . . . he could see her running in the mountains, running in the starlight where the grass was wet and the sun's coming as yet had not undone the rich matrix of creatures passed in the night before her. Deer and hare and dove and groundvole all richly empanelled on the air for her delight, all nations of the possible world ordained by God of which she was one among and not separate from. (*BT*, 436)

The apocalypse is no grandiose vision of angels and monsters and trumpets; it is a terminal disease that has eaten away the bones and fibers of a living language, since it can find no purchase in an animal "other," other than one that is already not just dead, but extinct. *The Road* clears a space for this language to sound, a *langue* without phoneme or articulation; nothing but a protracted rumble at best, at worst a howling silence. "Then a distant low rumble. Not thunder. You could feel it under your feet. A sound without cognate and so without description. Something imponderable shifting out there in the dark. The earth itself contracting with the cold. It did not come again. . . . The silence. The salitter drying from the earth." (279) "Perhaps in the world's destruction it would be possible at last to see how it was made. Oceans, mountains. The ponderous counterspectacle of things ceasing to be. The sweeping waste, hydroptic and coldly secular. The silence" (293). Extract the names of animals, and this "coldly secular" silence swallows up all creation. "Speechlessness: that is the great sorrow of nature." As Walter Benjamin noted: "God's creation is completed when things receive their names from man, from whom in name language alone speaks."[19] And it is uncompleted once things are again uncoupled from that language. In McCarthy's vision, too, the desolation of the world is a desolation of language, a rescinding of the sonorous names of mute things that bind a world into song.

In a restatement of a core theme of Benjamin, Eric Santner has this to say about the great critic's concept of "natural history," as what is stranded between historical forms of life and nature itself: "natural history is born out of the dual possibilities that life can persist beyond the death of the symbolic forms that gave it meaning and that symbolic forms can persist beyond the death of the form of life that gave them human vitality. Natural history transpires against the background of this space between real and symbolic death, this space of the 'undead.'"[20] The space of *The Road* is just such a space, where a creature roams having outlived the world-matrix of its being; and where the "sacred idiom" has become a fossilized linguistic bone, lodged in that creature's throat; a torment to truth.

Utopia, time, narration

Surely, these ruminations on origins and ends must have something to do with time itself and "our" collective inability to feel its innermost tensions today.[21] With the folding of the posthuman back into the prehuman around the central knot of the sacred beast, time recedes from the phenomenological frame: time, we could say, belonged to the *epoche* of the sacred, in a confirmation of the dialectical determination of the temporal by the eternal. The atemporal is something different again, not the sublation but the *extraction* of an entire Kantian categorical axis from the horizon of being. All that beckons now is space, an indefinite disclosure of what used to be an ontological opacity, but is now nothing but the endless drift of ash into the Beckettian "grey."[22] Time once *was*, but is now *not*, and the reason for that would seem to be that we have arrived at a certain Utopia [no-place]: blighted and forlorn, but utopic nonetheless, and chiefly for this extinguishment of the temporal flame.

Utopias, including the digital-global neoliberal one we inhabit, are where time goes to die. Relieved from the exhausting business of wresting freedom from necessity, the citizens of Utopia are as a rule also alleviated of the tribulations of temporality. In the positive Utopias—generically, long-winded descriptions of complex social formations in which nothing in particular seems to happen—time appears only as a vanishing point: the point of inauguration. "[A]s for the Event," writes Jameson, "it does indeed get registered, but as the mythic beginning of Utopian time, the moment of foundation or inauguration, the moment of revolutionary transition. All of diachronic time is compressed into this single apocalyptic instant, which the narrative relates as the memory of old people."[23] So it is in *The Road*, too, but negatively, in what surely cannot pass as an Orwellian "anti-Utopia" (since it does not concern itself with the evil perversions of affirmative state-building), or a "critical Utopia" (since it isn't concerned to test the existent against its innermost anti social tendencies), but can only be described by that haunted adjective, "apocalyptic." Symptomatically, the only reference to the inaugural punctum in this text immediately modulates from a temporal reference to a spatial one: "The clocks stopped at 1:17. A long shear of light and then a series of low concussions" (54). No doubt the "1:17" here is only ironically a reference to time, and assumes its true gravity as a chapter-and-verse reference to scripture, perhaps to the Book of Revelation, or the Epistle of James.

However, insofar as the text indicates an event in time, its reference is ghosted by an historical specificity that the book otherwise, in its allegorical distaste for all particulars, shrugs off. Namely, that "irreversible destruction" of all worldly coordinates, including, critically, those of the archive and thus of literature, that would be named by the phrase "nuclear war." It was Derrida who insisted that literature needed to be thought, under the sign of the nuclear event, as always-already mortal and exposed to death. The "death be not proud" of literature's many postures of immortality is undone by the nuclear age, to which deconstruction itself inevitably belonged:

> If "literature" is the name we give to the body of texts whose existence, possibility, and significance are the most radically threatened, for the first and last time, by the nuclear catastrophe, this gives one to think the essence of literature, its radical precariousness and the radical form of its historicity; but by the same token, through literature, what gives itself to thinking is the totality of that which, like literature and henceforth in it, is exposed to the same threat, constituted by the same structure of historical fictionality, producing and then harbouring its own referent.[24]

Nuclear war discloses not only literature's fragile self-destructibility (given its status as what is most disposed to an "essential finitude" by its reliance only upon its own archive—the "performative character of its relation to the referent," 402), but with it that of the world itself, as what too, finally, has no reference beyond its own immanence. The nuclear referent catalyzes an ontogenetic relationship between "literature" and "world." Establishing the real possibility, indeed the reality, of the death of literature, the nuclear event (whether or not it "happens") can only have made itself felt in and through literature's fictionality, figuration, symbolicity; it is what cannot be experienced outside of literary adumbrations. And in this dialectic, we can sense the "perspective of a remainderless destruction, without symbolicity, without memory, without mourning"—which is to say, we shudder to the absolute demise of world. For Derrida, literature has no greater, and no other vocation than to "assimilate this unassimilable wholly other" that is its own "remainderless and a-symbolic destruction"—its Real—and thus permit us to think the End, at last (403).

The Road, then, adduces this "nuclear" event to shatter time, and deliver us over to a space whose relationship to literature is that of a Utopian de-figuration. It is a book whose landscape consists of the ruins of other books:

> Years later he'd stood in the charred ruins of a library where blackened books lay in pools of water. Shelves tipped over. Some rage at the lies arranged in their thousands row on row.

He picked up one of the books and thumbed through the heavy bloated pages. He'd not have thought the value of the smallest thing predicated on a world to come. It surprised him. That the space which these things occupied was itself an expectation. He let the book fall and took a last look around and made his way out into the cold gray light. (199)

When the boy asks his father at one point, "There's not any crows. Are there?", he follows up the inevitable negation with the afterthought, "Just in books" (168), which don't exist either. It is only from a vantage point of literature's remainderless annihilation that the value of any book can stand revealed as promissory, as always and irrevocably "to come," even in its preservation of the names of non-existent things. What the books had vouchsafed was precisely world, more and more of it, a compendious extension of world in every direction, but above all into the open vector of time. This is related to the "bad infinity" or "bad eternity" of which Blanchot writes apropos of Borges, that man of the library for whom "the book is in principle the world. . ., and the world is a book."[25] Once we are without world, what becomes of all these book-worlds?

> . . .if the book is the possibility of the world, we should conclude that at work in the world is not only the ability to make [*faire*], but that great ability to feign [*feindre*], to trick and deceive, of which every work of fiction is the product, all the more so if this ability stays concealed in it. (94)

All the names of fiction stand accused by the Apocalypse of naming nothing. Such is finitude's revenge. The disaster is here, in literature's dangerous ability to go toward what exists by way of what does not; in the fragility of names, which are nothing, "precious remainders" without substance and without reference.

The very origins of the European novel as a modern form are whipped up in the apocalyptic storm; what McCarthy offers in *The Road* is an x-ray or diachronic cross-section of the phylogenetic history of that form in its death-throes, an unsteady and always potentially sterile fusion of the following generic layers: residual romance-adventure quest forms; picaresque; and the realism of individual travail made good by Defoe. And yet, within these irreducible elements of narrative generation and indications of origin, the narrator stubbornly refuses to record a single proper name (that isn't summarily retracted, as with the tramp "Ely"), or for that matter a single proper noun (apart from the well-nigh erotic charge of the single place name engraved on the sextant, "Hezzaninth, London," 243); so that the protagonists wander nameless through a nameless and uncoordinated space sapped of the charge of nominal pleasure that sustains novelistic narration. McCarthy shuttles the novel form back to a future in which human characters, having ceased to name those creatures that sustained the divine spark of their humanness, absorb that wretched namelessness into their own substance.

So it is that the space into which the work's conception of "natural history" leads it is perforce an allegorical space, just as Benjamin insisted of the *Trauerspiel*: "in allegory the observer is confronted with the *facies hippocratica* of history as a petrified, primordial landscape. Everything about history that, from the very beginning, has been untimely, sorrowful, unsuccessful, is expressed in a face—or rather in a death's head."[26] And that includes, essentially, literary history. The Utopia into which its "nuclear event" ushers this text is one of literature's own self-extinction, in which ruin, like a last flash of green on the horizon, its own genetic origins reappear in ghastly rigor mortis. Allegorizing its own allegory, here the subjection to death is absolute, and the book thus allows us to think "the totality of that which, like literature and henceforth in it, is exposed to the same threat"[27]: the world itself. But what still remains unthought is any articulation of this speculative dimension with a specific "politico-religious" history, which Benjamin's model of allegory urges us to acknowledge as part of its meaning (160). If the *Trauerspiel*'s history is that of the baroque, what is *The Road*'s?

Political amphibology of the "rightist" Utopia

Our initial thought is surely to calibrate the allegorical framework of this novel with, on the one hand, the reduction of American citizens to biopolitical "consumers" (Badiou's "capitalist nihilism" as what determines "the non-existence of any world"), and, on the other, the characteristic geopolitical situation of the so-called "excluded" (Badiou's "those who have no name").[28] In this case, the narrative of *The Road* would simultaneously express the "worldless" abandonment of the world's millions of refugees and asylum seekers to any number of territorialized sovereign exceptions *and* the apocalyptic posthumanity of a society prostrate before "a zombie system, seemingly dead when it comes to achieving human goals and responding to human feelings, but capable of sudden spurts of activity that cause chaos all around."[29] What we have thus far approached as a consequence of the post-sacredness of our linguistic substance, and the "nuclear event," would then disclose a global political dimension within which *homo sacer,* gravitating to either end of the biopolitical "animal humanism" of the day (see more below), was grasped as a *single* figure, an ambivalent allegorical locus.

But this tactic raises as many questions as it seems to settle, and displaces at least one pertinent political dimension internal to the text itself: namely, the level at which the relationship between Man and Boy instantiates the constitutional dialectic between State and Civil Society, or Sovereign and Subject. The father's unilateral judgments about preservation of the means of survival, and endorsement of a Schmittian political theology of "good guys" and "bad guys" (friends and enemies, where the friend never arrives), against the express wishes of his "civil society," would appear in the final moments of the text to have paradoxically been keeping at bay the non-cannibalistic commune into which the Boy is at last absorbed. The Man's "foreign policy" wards off the very thought of community thanks to a ubiquitous state of exception; but neither is this policy to be dismissed as unreasonable given the savagery into which the species as a whole has now degenerated. Here, other post-human hominids roam in a state not to be distinguished from those "primal hordes" ruled over by primal fathers in Freud's vision of the state of nature out of which civilized humanity eventually emerged (thanks in part to the inauguration of religious structures of feeling). And so it is that what first appeared as a workable allegory of Badiouesque "worldlessness" turns out to have been allegorizing, simultaneously, an intractable schism within the theory of the state, according to which *homo sacer* himself, given the minimal units of a political space (ruler, ruled), replicates the "sovereign exception" over his own polity. The number of times the Man broods over the unanswerable question, "Could you crush that beloved skull with a rock? Is there such a being within you of which you know nothing? Can there be?" (120), suggests the amphibology of all political allegories, which now appear Left, and now Right, according to what point on the revolving biopolitical wheel the eye stops to inspect.

It would be possible to read McCarthy's lifework as an eminently paradoxical evocation of a pointedly "rightist" frame of reference—hardened John-Fordian fringe-dwellers, given to their individualism, ringed round by violence, serially exposed to Evil, and surviving, if at all, in a diminished condition—whose larger (albeit silent) ideological plea would seem to be for the Big Other: *more law*. The exposed individual is violated in his innermost core by the absence of any legal safeguard. This is paradoxical principally in reference to the current state of the American Right, whose disavowals of all state interference, taxation and welfare as immanently totalitarian cannot easily be squared with the plangent sense of abandonment, spiritual and secular, that we get from McCarthy. It is less paradoxical when considered in the context of a more respectable American conservatism, which is animated by respect for the Constitution and a pragmatic tolerance of neighbors as the minimum requirement of a sense of community. Predating Reaganesque deregulation and neoliberalism as such, this quieter and more serene current of conservative thinking—which we probably tend to associate with the faces of Henry Fonda, Gary Cooper and, today, Clint Eastwood—is not predisposed to hysterical denunciations of the state. And yet, to the extent that McCarthy inhabits that tradition, neither could he be said to have taken any solace from the New Deal or Great Society, let alone any more avowedly redistributive statism: "There's no such thing as life without bloodshed," he has said in interview. "I think the notion that the species can be improved in some way, that everyone could live in harmony, is a really dangerous idea. Those who are afflicted with this notion are the first ones to give up their souls, their freedom."[30]

It is in this context, with the steady rise of Tea Party-esque anti-statism immediately behind it, that the equivocal anti-Utopianism of McCarthy's fictional worlds, culminating in *The Road*, needs to be understood. On the one hand, in tune with an old strand of frontier-dwelling Christianity, the species *homo sapiens* is presented as innately a fallen one, humanized only by a diet of bloodshed that willy-nilly increases the burden of its guilt; on the other, and given that very Hobbesian condition of *homo homini lupens*, minimal protection and safeguards would seem to be required to keep the beast of neighborly appetite from the door. The problem is one of figuration: how to avoid the "danger" of suggesting that, through state bodies and institutions, the human race might "improve" on its savage nature, while nevertheless demonstrating the terrible destinies awaiting an unchecked "human condition"? The fate of the kid in *Blood Meridian* is telling here. As Judge Holden increases his charismatic hold over the scalp-hunting Glanton gang, and the rate of primitive accumulation increases exponentially, the kid is ultimately driven to a *rapprochement* with state power in a San Diego prison: confessing the gang's crimes and setting out on an unremarkable maturity of wandering safe from harm, until the final reckoning. Yet the protection of the law neither extirpates the absolute Evil of the Judge, nor allows "the man" (as he now is) to enjoy any authentic existential depth. He is, as the Judge finally tells him, "a disappointment" (328), whereas the Judge himself, "his immense and terrible flesh" (333), seems to incarnate sovereign violence as the core of all human nature. The irresolvable tensions of the Western as a genre are as operative here as they are in any John Wayne film: the very law the narratives cry out for must be an existential disappointment at the level of narration. For McCarthy, the novel as a form finds its animus in a condition of nature that could never tolerate a novel inside it. The form itself is that against which the human element must take shelter from the pitiless storm of violence whipped up by what the form is struggling to master: the human element.

To that extent, the narrative universe of *The Road* can and must be taken as one sustained conservative "emblematic" of the essential fallenness of human nature, its innate depravity, into which the boy's radiance falls, meaninglessly, like Grace itself. So we have those prototypical visions of Freudian "primal hordes" shambling along the roads like the very incarnation of the death drive:

> They clanked past, marching with a swaying gait like wind-up toys. Bearded, their breath smoking through their masks. . . . Tramping. Behind them came wagons drawn by slaves in harness and piled with goods of war and after that the women, perhaps a dozen in number, some of them pregnant, and lastly a supplementary consort of catamites illclothed against the cold and fitted with dogcollars and yoked each to each. (96)

These creatures, along with their prey, are what human nature *is* in this conservative estimate: "the walking dead in a horror film." (57)

There is a zombie haunting America, a nation gone so thoroughly to the dogs that it can no longer discriminate friend from enemy. This zombie is something very different from what Eric Santner tries to articulate, after Benjamin, as the German-Jewish tradition of thought about "creaturely life": it is rather a perfectly conventional image of "man" as coterminous with his own animality. This is something that Alain Badiou particularly warns about in our ideological constellation:

> Considered in terms of its mere nature alone, the human animal must be lumped in the same category as its biological companions. This systematic killer pursues, in the giant ant hills he constructs, interests of survival and satisfaction neither more nor less estimable than those of moles or tiger beetles. He has shown himself to be the most wily of animals, the most patient, the most obstinately dedicated to the cruel desires of his own power.[31]

The net result of seeing the human being as just this biological triumph of ingenuity and cunning alone is a biopolitical hospice of "animal humanism," where what is inflicted on us as a self-image is the norm of the "victimized body": "the tortured, the massacred, the famished, the genocided. . . because man is no more than the animal datum of a body, whose most spectacular attestation . . . is suffering."[32] "Sooner or later they will catch us and they will kill us," the suicidal mother argues. "They will rape me. They'll rape him. They are going to rape us and kill us and eat us and you wont face it." (58) Happening upon a Carolinian mansion that is itself a time-machine articulating post history with the Federation's political conception in its compromises over slavery, Boy and Man discover these victims in the basement: "naked people, male and female, all trying to hide" from the cannibal horde living off their flesh (116).

The question arises again: if this is what we posthumans have become, what could possibly save us from our own unchecked animal appetites? What law might protect us from our own savagery? The rote answer of animal humanism today is the universal law of human rights: a biopolitical regime of species domestication that accepts this animal for what it is, and administers its life accordingly. When you look into the face of your own offspring and see this, you are already awaiting the jeeps of the NGOs: "He looked like something out of a deathcamp. Starved, exhausted, sick with fear"

(123). The aggressive recrudescence in our time of this disabused and brutally realist conception of "human nature" plays directly to the hand of neoliberal governance, about which Jameson once wrote these salient words:

> For the authoritarian regimes today are based on at least a grudging consent, a deep instinctive feeling that law and order must be the first priority, along with "fiscal restraint," and that a certain firmness is necessary. . ... Such regimes . . . finally prove to be based on a renewed conception of human nature as something sinful and aggressive that demands to be held in check for its own good (and for that of those who govern it); power here coming to be justified in the name of the doctrine of the secret will to power of all ameliorative social movements. Even the left—certainly the liberal centre—has largely capitulated to the resignation of this disabused view of the human animal. . . .[33]

We have said that McCarthy's aesthetic imagination and ideology come up short before this avowal of state power and biopolitical management as the solution to the barbaric capacities of the human animal that he depicts so cathartically. He is, to that extent, in flight from any affirmative depictions of the "firmness" that would take the suffering of *homo sacer* in hand and build for it an ark to weather the flood of blood and ordure. This is why his Utopia is a negative one: neither liberal nor radical, but a right-wing Apocalypse. What rescues it from outright nihilism is the feeble rays of grace that now and then fall across the ashen surfaces of the text. Like Badiou, intriguingly, McCarthy too believes that "*by grace*, this particular animal is sometimes seized by something that thought cannot manage to reduce strictly to the thought of animality as such."[34] It is just that, far from being conjured from the evental site of a situation's void, McCarthy's grace is forced into presentation from the domain of animality itself.

Style as (minor) event

To detect the outline of grace in this book, it pays to heed the critical difference between the ways in which the man and the boy seize their de-nominated space, and dispose themselves toward it. It is most often simply a matter of grammatical aptitudes. Time and again, what passes for their conversation reveals itself as a virtual *différend* (in Lyotard's sense) between two irreconcilable axiomatics at the level of grammar. First, the man, who inhabits his dying language and the falling away of names from things in a melancholy state, deploys all his verbal energies in an imperative mood, the *have to* and *don't* and *can't* forms of insistence, as if to counteract the wistfulness of his own nostalgia and his mounting despair. And second, against this, a perpetually resisting force, the boy's openly subjunctive and optative moods, his tone and tense always interrogative, conditional, uncertain, forward-reaching and beseeching.

> What if there's someone here, Papa?
> There's no one here.
> We should go, Papa.
> We've got to find something to eat. We have no choice.
> We could find something somewhere else.
> It's going to be all right. Come on. (122)

There are two ways of inhabiting a dying language. Either force it up against the inevitable in harsh and unbending imperatives; or find auxiliary verbs like *could* and *might* and *ought*, that yield to the namelessness only to pluck from it some unguessed at latency, some "somewhere else" that is dimly imaginable, despite figuring nothing forth. Utopia resides in the grain of the grammar: "Do we know where Mars is? . . . If we had a spaceship could we go there?" (166) The agon of *The Road* is between these two linguistic dispositions; one of them terminal, the other immortal.

But where they finally become decisive is not at the level of dialogue or the *différend* implicit in it. What becomes clearer and clearer is that, while his spoken discourse with the boy is reduced to the role of a survivalist sovereign decked out in the imperative, the man's inner life—where the temporal dimension ticks like an undetonated bomb—is disposed very differently. And just as the dialogical agon is fleshed out through the aporetic dyad of man and boy, this inner depth is chiseled out by the dialectic between the man and his narrator. Indeed, the free-indirect discursive zone charged by the friction between this character and the narrator can be seen as the inverted, *camera obscura* image of the man's relationship with his son: for here, it is the man who holds out against the brutal assurances of the narrator that all is dead and dying, and that, fundamentally, nothing is. In the free-indirect discursive space, the Man's imperative sovereignty is transposed into the narrator's calm indicativeness with regard to the fate of things; whereas the Boy's yearning conditionals and subjunctive mood are transfigured into the past tense of anterior life (inaccessible to the Boy himself), where they set off resonant depth charges. It is, indeed, within the sealed cave of memory that these "future anterior" accesses of sheer memory—memory with the force of an event, a material remainder capable of reconfiguring the space of perception—are discharged by a language now freighted with much more than pitiless indicativeness. Memory here has the sacrificial force of the sacred. "He thought each memory recalled must do some violence to its origins. . . . So be sparing." (139)

How, in a literary space as restricted as this one, to afford the reader a mnemonic dream-glimpse, however imaginary, of the *good life* as this will have left some faint negative trace on the burned-out shells of posthumanity? How, in other words, to "bring out the utopia in the negative picture"?[35] To what are the boy's various optative verbal strainings—like so many adjustments of radio antennae to non-existent signals in the ether—attuned? Where is this absurd upsurge of hope ultimately to be tempered into the tensile aesthetic web of an image, given that the substrate of all images is now perished? The answer, of course, will concern animals, since animals are indeed the teachers of the only image of happiness we are permitted to know:

> *Rien faire comme une bête*, lying on water and looking peacefully at the sky, "being, nothing else, without any further definition and fulfilment," might take the place of process, act, satisfaction, and so truly keep the promise of dialectical logic that it would culminate in its origin.[36]

We have seen already the apocalyptic force of the opening image of the white beast; but now a whole network of animal imagery is lit up by linguistic grace. "There was a lingering odor of cows in the barn and he stood there thinking about cows and he realized they were extinct. Was that true? There could be a cow somewhere being fed and cared for, Could there? Fed what? Saved for what?" (127) But this is not yet an exercise in style; it is the mere suggestion of a subject. Again using an unwonted subjunctive form, the narrator later tells us: "He thought there could be . . . life in the deep. Great squid propelling themselves over the floor of the sea in the cold darkness. Shuttling past like trains, eyes the size of saucers." (234) Here picking up the lost rhythm of an abandoned project (that of the American Renaissance: to name its world), and transposing it to Melvillian submarine opacities, the narrator is provoked to the absurd practice of making similes in which neither term exists. Style "begins again" where the animal's ink has stained the liquid element of thought. Then, penultimately, this:

> Standing at the edge of a winter field among rough men. The boy's age. A little older. Watching while they opened up the rocky hillside ground with pick and mattock and brought to light a great bolus of serpents perhaps a hundred in number. Collected there for a common warmth. The dull tubes of them beginning to move sluggishly in the cold hard light. Like the bowels of some great beast exposed to the day. The men poured gasoline on them and burned them alive, having no remedy for evil but only for the image of it as they conceived it to be. The burning snakes twisted horribly and some crawled burning across the floor of the grotto to illuminate its darker recesses. As they were mute there were no screams of pain and the men watched them burn and writhe and blacken in just such silence themselves and they disbanded in silence in the winter dusk each with his own thoughts to go home to their suppers. (200–1)

With the mute cry of all nature condensed into a single writhing figure of serpentine agony, the narrator has virtually liberated what it is at work in the memory of the man that might go by the name of the sacred. Virtually, but not quite. For here we are still within the sacrificial logic of Faulkner and Hemingway, according to which gods can be conjured at their vanishing point in blood sport. To the extent that this passage remains mortgaged to sacrifice, it has not yet instantiated the god of this book, which awaits the termination of all narrative interest for its appearance. Of course, its apparition can only have been negative, under the sign of extinction (like all the others); but at last, having survived the numerous taxonomic, stylistic, and descriptive mortifications of the book's puritanical economy, it can speak its name.

Once there were brook trout in the streams in the mountains. You could see them standing in the amber current where the white edges of their fins wimpled softly in the flow. They smelled of moss in your hand. Polished and muscular and torsional. On their backs were vermiculate patterns that were maps of the world in its becoming. Maps and mazes. Of a thing which could not be put back. Not be made right again. In the deep glens where they lived all things were older than man and they hummed of mystery. (306–7)

Notes

1   On this concept, see Daniel Zalewski, "The Ecstatic Truth: Werner Herzog's Quest," *The New Yorker* (April 24, 2006), accessed at http://www.newyorker.com/archive/2006/04/24/060424fa_fact_zalewski on 10/20/11.

2   Theodor Adorno and Max Horkheimer, *Dialectic of Enlightenment*, trans. John Cumming (London & New York: Verso, 1986), p. 15.

3   Giorgio Agamben, *The Open: Man and Animal*, trans. Kevin Attell (Stanford CA: Stanford University Press, 2004), p. 16.

4   Martin Heidegger, "Language," in *Poetry, Language, Thought*, trans. Albert Hofstadter, new edition (New York: Harper Perennial, 1976), p. 197.

5   Ralph Waldo Emerson, "Literary Ethics," c.1838, in *Essays and Lectures*, ed. J. Porte (New York: Library of America, 1983), p. 101.

6   Henry David Thoreau, *Walden and Civil Disobedience* (New York & London: Penguin, 1983), p. 332–3.

7   Walt Whitman, "Specimen Days," in *Poetry and Prose*, ed. J. Kaplan (New York: Library of America, 1996), p. 812.

8   See Herman Melville, Chapter 87, "The Grand Armada," *Moby-Dick; or, The Whale*, ed. H. Beaver (London: Penguin, 1972), pp. 487–501.

9   Walter Benjamin, *The Origin of German Tragic Drama*, trans. John Osborne (London & New York: Verso, 1985), pp. 224–5.

10 "He made the earth first and peopled it with dumb creatures, and then He created man to be his overseer on the earth and to hold suzerainty over the earth and the animals on it in His name, not to hold for himself and his descendants inviolable title forever, generation after generation, to the oblongs and squares of the earth, but to hold the earth mutual and intact in the communal anonymity

of brotherhood, and all the fee He asked was pity and humility
and sufferance and endurance and the sweat of his face for bread."
William Faulkner, "The Bear," in *The Portable Faulkner*, revised and
expanded ed. ed. M. Cowley (New York & London: Penguin, 2003),
p. 229.

11 Ernest Hemingway, *The Essential Hemingway* (London: Panther,
1977), p. 341.

12 Thoreau, *Walden*, p. 133.

13 "Each portion of matter may be conceived as like a garden full of
plants and like a pond full of fishes. But each branch of every plant,
each member of every animal, each drop of its liquid parts is also
some such garden or pond." See Gottfried Wilhelm Leibniz, *The
Monadology*, 67.

14 Cormac McCarthy, *Blood Meridian, Or the Evening Redness in the
West* (London: Picador, 1990), pp. 316–17.

15 Cormac McCarthy, *The Border Trilogy* (London: Picador, 2007), p. 870.

16 Thoreau, *Walden*, pp. 328–9.

17 The obscurity of this word, unmentioned by the *OED*, is apt in
context; used by seventeenth-century mystic Jakob Boehme (after
Seton and Helbach) to designate the germinal spiritual substance of
paradise, the word has lapsed entirely from use and knowledge. See
Andrew Weeks, *Boehme: An Intellectual Biography* (Albany, NY:
SUNY Press, 1991), pp. 65–7.

18 Animal language is a major concern of Cary Wolfe's *What is
Posthumanism* (Minneapolis: University of Minnesota Press, 2010).

19 Walter Benjamin, "On Language as Such and the Language of Man,"
trans. Edmund Jephcott, in *Selected Writings, Volume 1: 1913–26*, ed.
M. Bullock, M. W. Jennings (Cambridge, MA: The Belknap Press of
Harvard University Press, 2004), 72, 65.

20 Eric Santner, *On Creaturely Life: Rilke, Benjamin, Sebald* (Chicago
and London: University of Chicago Press, 2006), p. 17.

21 On this, see Fredric Jameson, "The End of Temporality," *Critical
Inquiry* 29.4 (Summer 2003): 695–718.

22 See Chris Danta's essay in this volume.

23 Jameson, *Archaeologies of the Future: The Desire Called Utopia and
Other Science Fictions* (London & New York: Verso, 2005), p. 187.

24 Jacques Derrida, "No Apocalypse, Not Now," in *Psyche: Inventions
of the Other*, Volume 1, ed. P. Kamuf, E. Rottenberg, trans. Catherine
Porter and Philip Lewis (Stanford: Stanford University Press, 2007),
pp. 400–1.

25 Maurice Blanchot, *The Book to Come*, trans. Charlotte Mandel
(Stanford: Stanford University Press, 2003), p. 94.

26 Benjamin, *Origin of German Tragic Drama*, p. 166.

27 Derrida, *op. cit.*

28 See Alain Badiou, *Polemics*, trans. Steve Corcoran (London & New York: Verso, 2006), 34.

29 Chris Harman, *Zombie Capitalism: Global Crisis and the Relevance of Marx* (Chicago: Haymarket Books, 2010), p. 12.

30 Quoted in Richard B. Woodward, "Cormac McCarthy's Venomous Fiction," *New York Times Books Review* (April 19, 1992).

31 Alain Badiou, *Ethics: An Essay on the Understanding of Evil*, trans. Peter Hallward (London & New York: Verso, 2002), pp. 58–9. See Mark Steven's essay in this volume.

32 Badiou, *The Century*, trans. Alberto Toscano (Cambridge: Polity, 2007), p. 175.

33 Jameson, *The Seeds of Time* (New York: Columbia University Press, 1994), p. 49.

34 Badiou, *Ethics*, p. 133.

35 Max Horkheimer in Adorno and Horkheimer, *Towards a New Manifesto*, p. 62.

36 Adorno, *Minima Moralia: Reflections from Damaged Life*, trans. E. F. N. Jephcott (New York & London: 2005), p. 167.

8

McCarthy's fire

PAUL PATTON

There are many ways one could say what *The Road* is about. It might be described as a story about the relationship between a father and his son, under the most extreme conditions; or as a story about the fragility of all that we regard as essential to living a human life; or even as an account set after the rapture, focusing on the tribulations leading up the second coming of Christ.[1] I propose to consider it, first, as a reflection on the nature of events, or on the very conditions of there being events in the world, and second, as a reflection on the nature of morality in world without God.

The Road is set in the aftermath of an unexplained event. It imagines a world in which something unidentified and perhaps unidentifiable has already taken place. This catastrophic event inaugurated a world in which the conditions of civilized life have all been destroyed. There are no longer public utilities that provide power, water, or means of communication and transport, let alone the institutions of government that preserve a measure of personal security. Not only the social but also the natural world has been stripped bare: forests have been reduced to dead tree trunks, animal life is extinguished even from the rivers and lakes, surface water everywhere blackened with ash and debris. The effects of fire are omnipresent:

> The ashes of the late world carried on the bleak and temporal winds to and fro in the void. Carried forth and scattered and carried forth again. Everything uncoupled from its shoring. (9)

Entire cities have been incinerated, their fleeing populations trapped and burnt in vehicles along the road, their buildings broken and ransacked of anything that might sustain human life. The novel is set a few years after the unnamed and unexplained catastrophe took place. In that time, the moral as well as the material infrastructure of society has been torn away. All that remains is a *Mad Max* world of roaming bands in search of ever diminishing supplies of canned or dried food. Worse still, in the absence of any living animals, they hunt for other people. *The Road* recounts the journey of a boy and his father along what remains of an interstate highway through the desolate burnt-out landscape somewhere in the Southeastern United States, heading south toward the sea and the hope of a warmer climate. Rather than live on in such a world confronted with the daily risk of being caught, raped, killed, and eaten, the child's mother preferred to end her own life with a sharpened stone. The father and son travel alone through this most primitive state of nature in which man has literally become wolf to man: "The frailty of everything revealed at last." (24)

We are never told what happened. A single sentence describes the father's first awareness of the enigmatic occurrence that inaugurated this new world: "A long shear of light and then a series of low concussions." (45) Some readers take this to indicate a nuclear holocaust, which would imply that the disaster was of human origin and possibly even the result of a conflict of civilizations and religions. But there is no mention of radiation and at one point the father and son discover a bunker that might have been a fallout shelter but was never used by its owners. Other scenarios are equally plausible, such as global warming or a large extra-terrestrial body that would have exploded on impact, causing a massive dust cloud that would have suddenly cooled the earth. These are not man-made events but rather suggest nature's complete indifference to the conditions of human existence. Whatever the cause, the effect was firestorms and a cloud of ash that have rendered the earth no longer able to sustain animal or eventually human life.

The result is a world in which, not only do we not know what has happened, but in which the very conditions of ever doing so are beginning to fade away. Books have become no more than material for fires. Memories and even the names of things from the world before have become increasingly difficult to recall. McCarthy describes it as a world in which human life has been reduced to the barest essentials of nourishment, shelter and personal safety:

The world shrinking down about a raw core of parsible entities. The names of things slowly following those things into oblivion. Colors. The names of birds. Things to eat. Finally the names of things one believed to be true. More fragile than he would have thought. How much was gone already? The sacred idiom shorn of its referents and so of its reality. Drawing down like something trying to preserve heat. In time to wink out forever. (75)

The epithet "survivors" is twice refused, or denied, to those who live on in this wasteland. In order for them to be survivors, there would have to be some event that had been survived and some meaningful life from which they could look back on what had happened. However, as the passage quoted above suggests, the characters in this novel confront the imminent death of all meaning and with this the very possibility of there being events.

The hermeneutical sublime

McCarthy's novel presents us with an event that exemplifies the conditions that make unexpected catastrophic events so terrifying, especially in the initial aftershock, namely that we do not know how to describe, identify, or name the event. As a result, we do not *know* what it is that has happened. Jacques Derrida suggests that this was what made September 11 such an overwhelming event, namely the considerable damage wrought upon

> the conceptual, semantic, and one could even say hermen-
> eutic apparatus that might have allowed one to see coming,
> to *comprehend*, interpret, describe, speak of, and name
> 'September 11.'[2]

Events of this kind are sublime but in a sense that, following Derrida's characterization of what makes it possible to identify and describe them as a "hermeneutic apparatus," we can call the hermeneutical sublime. The hermeneutical sublime is not mentioned in Kant's typology of ways of experiencing the sublime, but it is entirely consistent with his conception of the mental faculties. We can understand the experience of this kind of sublimity as produced by those phenomena that threaten to overwhelm not just our powers of imagination or physical resistance but also our capacity to understand or identify the phenomena in question. There would then be three different kinds of sublime, each one corresponding to one of the primary faculties: the mathematical sublime would be an effect of unimaginability in relation to the senses or the faculty of intuition; the dynamical sublime would be an effect of the incorruptibility of the will or the faculty of desire; and the hermeneutical sublime would be an effect of the limits of the intellect or the faculty of understanding.

Consider Kant's discussion of the different kinds of sublimity in the *Critique of the Power Judgment*. The "mathematical sublime" is the feeling aroused in us by those appearances of nature "the intuition of which brings with them the idea of their infinity."[3] The night sky, for example, with its immeasurable host of galaxies and stars, confronts our imagination with an impossible task of comprehension that exceeds the capacity of the imagination to represent the whole in a single mental image. For Kant, this incapacity has to do with the fact that the faculty of imagination must produce an image or "intuition" by means of a series of successive syntheses of momentary intuitions. It follows that, whenever we are faced with the possibility of an infinite series of such syntheses, the task lies beyond the powers of a finite imagination. By contrast, the human faculty of reason has no difficulty in thinking the idea of infinity. Only reason can encompass the entire universe as it extends through space and time, not in a whole of intuition but in an Idea of reason. According to Kant, the peculiar pleasure of the mathematical sublime derives from the manner in which the interminable effort to imagine an infinite whole inevitably leads our mind from the incapacity of the finite imagination to the infinite capacity of reason. The experience of the mathematical sublime is thus produced by thinking those phenomena that, by their very nature, provide evidence of "a faculty of the mind that surpasses every measure of the senses."[4]

The dynamical sublime is produced in us by those appearances of nature's might and power that are so overwhelming that the prospect of human resistance to them is inconceivable. In this manner,

> Bold, overhanging, as it were threatening cliffs, thunder clouds towering up into the heavens, bringing with them flashes of lightning and crashes of thunder, volcanos with their

all-destroying violence, hurricanes with the devastation they leave behind, the boundless ocean set into a rage, a lofty waterfall on a mighty river, etc., make our capacity to resist into an insignificant trifle in comparison with their power. But the sight of them only becomes all the more attractive the more fearful it is, as long as we find ourselves in safety, and we gladly call these objects sublime because they elevate the strength of our soul above its usual level, and allow us to discover within ourselves a capacity for resistance of quite another kind, which gives us the courage to measure ourselves against the apparent all-powerfulness of nature.[5]

This power of resistance within us is of course the human will that, as Kant points out elsewhere, is characterized by its freedom from determination by any sensible or material desires. As in the case of the mathematical sublime, the pleasure that is produced by such experiences is an indirect or "negative" pleasure involving a complex activity of repulsion-attraction produced in the mind. The first phase of this double movement is a perception of the overwhelming and inconceivable force of nature, before which our own physical power of resistance is nothing more than "a trifling moment." At this stage, we confront an incomprehensible power, a potential threat to our lives and projects before which resistance is, in a broad sense of the term, unimaginable. The second phase in this experience of sublimity, and the real source of the pleasure involved, involves the reassuring rediscovery of the capacity of the human will to resist every natural power. Whereas in the case of the mathematical sublime it is the power of human reason revealed in response to the incapacity of the imagination that gives rise to a kind of pleasure, here it is rather the power of the human will to remain unyielding even in the face of threats to our very existence:

the irresistibility of [nature's] power certainly makes us, considered as natural beings, recognize our physical powerlessness, but at the same time it reveals a capacity for judging ourselves as independent of it and a superiority over nature on which is grounded a self-preservation of quite another kind than that which can be threatened and endangered by nature outside us, whereby the humanity in our person remains undemeaned even though the human being must submit to that dominion.[6]

In this manner, we are reminded of our capacity to hold fast to principles of reason and thereby saved from the "humiliation" that would result if we were shown to be mere commonplace inhabitants of the natural world, no different from the vulgar animals.

The hermeneutical sublime would be the feeling produced in us by phenomena or events so foreign to our conceptual apparatus that we do not know how to describe them, or by the kind of world that McCarthy imagines in which the names of things follow the things themselves into oblivion. This is the feeling that he attempts to convey in the passage cited above, a feeling that the father had had before "beyond the numbness and the dull despair." (75) Derrida generalizes the hermeneutically sublime dimension of events in suggesting that every event, to the extent that it is an event and therefore a new occurrence at a given moment in time, implies a form of resistance to our existing representational systems or hermeneutic apparatus:

> The event is what comes and, in coming, comes to surprise me, to surprise and to suspend comprehension: the event is first of all *that which* I do not first of all comprehend. Better, the event is first of all *that* I do not comprehend. It consists in *that*, *that* I do not comprehend: *that which* I do not comprehend and first of all *that* I do not comprehend, the fact that I do not comprehend: my incomprehension.[7]

In other words, in order for there to be an event there must be recognition, identification, interpretation, or description of a given occurrence as a certain kind of event. At the same time, however, to the extent that an event is a new occurrence, it must also be endowed with the potential to resist this "appropriation" by or within our existing systems of recognition, representation, and comprehension. In this sense, every event carries within itself the potential to be unimaginable to greater or lesser extent. Every event, in so far as it is an event, carries the potential to break with the past and to inaugurate a new kind of event. This element of the unimaginable implicit in every event lies behind Derrida's suggestion that

> The ordeal of the event has as its tragic correlate not what is presently happening or what has happened in the past but the

precursory signs of what threatens to happen. It is the future that determines the unappropriability of the event, not the present or the past.[8]

It is for this reason, he suggests, that the terrifying character of the events of September 11 needs to be understood less against the background of the past or what actually happened, than against the background of what this event portends for the future.[9] If this kind of unexpected attack on ordinary citizens is possible, so might be a chemical, bacteriological or even nuclear attack. In other words, the traumatic character of the events of September 11 derives not just from what has happened but also from what might yet happen. The powerful impact of these events upon the political imaginary derives from the threat that, however bad they were, there may worse to come. It is this implicit threat of an even larger catastrophe that lies behind the fascination and horror aroused by September 11.

But these possible future catastrophic attacks do not fully exhaust the sense in which, for Derrida, September 11 was an unintelligible or sublime event, for they are entirely conceivable extrapolations of events that have already taken place. They remain within the bounds of what might occur as a matter of technological and political possibility. They are only *relatively* inconceivable, in the sense that they remain within the limits of what we have experienced up to now or what we can conceive as possible today. For Derrida, the occurrence of any event and the sense in which it implies the possibility of resistance to our systems of conceptualization and description is inescapably bound up with what he calls the "absolute future," by which he means the indeterminate, open, and paradoxical future that is the condition of there being events properly so called at all. This is what he refers to as elsewhere as the "to come," understood as "the space opened in order for there to be an event, the to-come, so that the coming be that of the other."[10] While it is this absolute future that ensures that there is an element of the inconceivable, and therefore the sublime, in every event, the prospect of even more horrific terrorist attacks are not *absolutely* inconceivable. For that there must be some completely unrecognizable occurrence, something that we would not see coming and that will have been so unexpected and unidentifiable that we cannot even be sure what it was that took place. This is precisely the kind of pure event that McCarthy presents us with in *The Road*.

Morality in a world without God

At the heart of *The Road* is the story of the father's effort to imbue
his son with the most rudimentary elements of a moral code. He tries
to tell him inspirational stories of courage and justice and to instill
in him a simple morality that, in the end, reduces to the difference
between the bad guys, who eat human flesh, and the good guys
who don't. At one point, after discovering people in the cellar of
a house who have been captured and kept alive even after having
been partly butchered, the son asks his father:

> We wouldn't ever eat anybody, would we?
> No. Of course not.
> Even if we were starving?
> . . ...
> No. No matter what.
> Because we're the good guys.
> Yes.
> And we're carrying the fire.
> And we're carrying the fire. Yes. (108–9)

Earlier, this belief that they are carrying the fire is associated with
the child's conviction that nothing bad is going to happen to them.
The belief that they are the good guys is explicitly linked to the
existence of God when the father says that his job is to take care of
the child and that he was appointed to do this by God. (80) Along
the road, they meet an old blind man who says, although he later
denies, that his name is Ely (short for Elijah, the Old Testament
prophet who raised the dead, brought down fire from the sky and
ascended to heaven in a whirlwind) who tells them that he always
believed that something like this would happen. He also tells them
that there are no gods: "Where man cant live gods fare no better."
(145) Even the primitive religions of ancestor worship are declared
false by the narrator in a passage that recalls Nietzsche's genealogy
of bad conscience:

> Do you think that your fathers are watching? That they weigh
> you in their ledgerbook? Against what? There is no book and
> your fathers are dead in the ground. (165)

What are we to make of the infantile moral tale of the good guys and the bad guys and what does the fire supposedly carried by the man and his son amount to? One way to approach these issues is via the difference between a naturalistic and a supernaturalistic conception of the human condition. For Kant, it is human freedom and the possibility of moral judgment that saves humanity from the "total humiliation" that would result from perpetual subservience to the demands of physical survival. Indeed, on his account, the experience of the sublime is endowed with moral significance to the extent that it reminds us of the "supersensible" character of human reason and will. The dynamic sublime is especially significant from a moral point of view since it reminds us of the human capacity to hold fast to rational principles for action in the face of the most extreme threats to the very existence of our sensible being. By contrast, from Nietzsche's thoroughly naturalistic and historical perspective on the human animal, this is a "monstrous method of evaluation" that denies the conditions and value of human life.[11] Kant's account of the means by which mortal humans are saved from "humiliation" at the hands of overwhelming natural forces exemplifies the primary nihilism that Nietzsche diagnoses as the wellspring of the ascetic ideal that has informed so much of European culture. It supposes that we are not merely natural beings inhabiting the sensible realm of natural phenomena, but also supersensible beings inhabiting an intelligible realm by virtue of the faculties of reason and will that ensure our "pre-eminence" over nature. Nietzsche regards this nihilism as the most important obstacle to a future state of humanity in which other modes of evaluation will prevail. *Thus Spoke Zarathustra* is his dramatic prophecy of the possibility of a different type of human being, without ressentiment at the natural conditions of life, including death, and with no need of supersensible worlds behind the natural world to ensure an imaginary pre eminence over life itself.

Many passages in *The Road* draw attention to the kind of natural phenomena that return us to the first moment of Kant's dynamic sublime. The man and his son encounter a waterfall, an earthquake, extreme darkness and, at one point, a low rumbling sound as though the earth itself was contracting with the cold. (220) But McCarthy's version of the hermeneutic sublime presents us with a much bleaker world. One morning, the father walks out into the grey light and sees

. . . for a brief moment the absolute truth of the world. The cold
relentless circling of the intestate earth. Darkness implacable.
The blind dogs of the sun in their running. The crushing black
vacuum of the universe. (110)

The second moment of Kant's dynamic sublime, the comforting
belief in the "supersensible" character of human existence, is
entirely absent from this world. If it is present at all in the novel,
this is only in the form of a conflict between the human imaginary
that sustained life in the old world and the conditions of life in the
new. The structure of the dynamic sublime is present as it were in
relief, in the form of a tension between what the nameless father
and some other adults would like to able to continue to believe
and what the narrative voice and the narrative itself suggest it is
possible to believe in this godless world. Their journey to the sea
does not lead the man and his son to a promised land but only to
more devastation:

At the tide line a woven mat of weeds and the ribs of fishes
in their millions stretching along the shore as far as eye could
see like an isocline of death. One vast salt sepulchre. Senseless.
Senseless. (187)

Read against the background of the absence of meaning or referent
for "the sacred idiom" of the world as it had been before the
unnameable event, the fire carried by the father and his son in *The
Road* might be read as a substitute for the belief in a supernatural
God that had hitherto sustained European morality. The fire is a
symbol that, in the stripped down morality passed on from father to
son, plays the role that had formerly been played by what Nietzsche
called the "afterworld": the world behind the world that is the
essential component of the ascetic ideal in all its forms. As such,
this fire recalls the fire that is described at the end of *No Country
for Old* Men, when the aging sheriff recounts a dream to his uncle.
In it, he sees his father one night when the two of them were riding
through a pass in the mountains:

It was cold and there was snow on the ground and he rode past
me and kept on goin. Never said nothin. He just rode on past and
he had this blanket wrapped around him and he had his head
down and when he rode past I seen he was carryin fire in a horn

the way people used to do and I could see the horn from the light inside of it. About the colour of the moon. And in the dream I knew that he was goin on ahead and that he was fixin to make a fire somewhere out there in all that dark and cold and I knew that whenever I got there he would be there. And then I woke up.[12]

The significance of this fire is expressed in the penultimate sentence. It embodies the comforting belief that we are not alone in the dark and cold universe, and that somewhere out there in time and space there is light and warmth waiting for us at the end of the journey.[13] *The Road* is a particularly vivid depiction of such a dark and cold universe, and the simple morality that the father passes on to his son in the end comes down to the belief that there is such light and warmth and that, because there is, there are some things people should not do to one another. The old sheriff in *No Country* presents the rationale for this kind of stripped-down moral code when he says

> I think the truth is always simple. It has pretty much got to be. It needs to be simple enough for a child to understand. Otherwise it'd be too late. By the time you figured it out it would be too late. (249)

For the old sheriff, the truth is simple in ways that arguably expose the limitations of his version of it. For example, when he responds to the liberal case for abortion with the argument that if this is allowed so will be the killing of the old and the infirm. (197) As though there were not circumstances in which people might not prefer to be killed rather than go on suffering. The sheriff's fire is perhaps still too close to the comforting father figure of some versions of Christian religion. He admits at one point that he has waited eighty some years for God to come into his life. (283) The fire in *The Road* is less specific. It is no more than the light of an ideal or belief that supports some rules, some limits to what people are prepared to do to others and therefore to themselves in order to stay alive. Is it possible to provide an interpretation of the fire that distinguishes it from the limited perspective of the sheriff and even from what Nietzsche calls the ascetic ideal embodied in the belief in a divine world behind the world of the senses? Can we distinguish the need to have rules from the particular rules that have governed moral judgment and behavior in a particular form of society?

The question of the meaning of this fire is raised by the final sentence of *No Country* where, after recounting the dream involving his father and the fire, the Sheriff says that he woke up. In *The Road*, too, the belief in afterworlds is assimilated to a dream that expresses only the fact that the dreamer has given up on life:

> When your dreams are of some world that never was or of some world that never will be and you are happy again then you will have given up. Do you understand? And you cant give up. I wont let you. (160)

So is the aspiration expressed in McCarthy's fire simply a comforting illusion that human beings need to be able to live and to set limits to their behavior? Or is it more than that, a necessary illusion perhaps but one that can be understood as more than just the expression of nihilism, of giving up on life. Is it rather a way of coming to terms with our condition of being alone in a dark and cold universe. Even Nietzsche recognized the need to provide some alternative to the ascetic ideal: the "truth" of eternal return can be read as providing another standard for judging one's actions, a non punitive standard without ressentiment.

In these terms, we might understand the fire in *The Road* as a metaphor for some kind of moral order and as such the guarantee of a future humanity that is clearly intended, at least in the eyes of the father to be borne by the son. That it is difficult for the father to think outside the terms of the sacred idiom is evident in the manner in which the boy is at times imbued with Christ-like qualities of concern for others, innocence, and even "a light all about him." (223) At the end of the novel, the father dies and the boy is taken in by a family of presumed good guys who speak the language of the divinity of the old world. However, we do not know whether they or the boy will survive, let alone what kind of man he will become.

The final paragraph returns us to a nature that is indifferent to man in that it is made up of things that were "older than man" and that "hummed of mystery." Patterns on the back of mountain trout are "maps of the world its own becoming." (241) We can take this to suggest the possibility of a world without humans, but we can also suppose that the boy represents not so much the messiah as the possibility of a genuine metamorphosis of the human animal. He is like the child whose coming is announced at the end of *Thus Spoke*

Zarathustra: the first of Zarathustra's children, an indication or sign that humanity in its present and past incarnations will be succeeded by an "overhuman" being freed of ressentiment and the ascetic ideal that ministered to this sickness. This is the truly unimaginable future event alluded to by the novel. In one sense of the term, the catastrophic and world-transforming event that has taken place is all too conceivable and therefore imaginable. In other sense, the future humanity that genuinely will have survived such a catastrophe remains profoundly and irreducibly unimaginable. That is why, shortly before the father dies, he sees the boy "standing there in the road looking back at him from some unimaginable future . . ." (231)

Notes

1 Carl James Grindley, "The Setting of McCarthy's *The Road*," *The Explicator,* 67 (Winter 2008): 11–13.
2 Jacques Derrida, "Autoimmunity: Real and Symbolic Suicides" in *Philosophy in a Time of Terror*, ed. G. Borradori (Chicago and London: University of Chicago Press, 2003), 93 (emphasis added).
3 Immanuel Kant, *The Critique of the Power of Judgment* (5: 255), trans. Paul Guyer and Eric Matthews, Cambridge: Cambridge University Press, 2000, 138.
4 Kant, *The Critique of the Power of Judgment* (5: 250), 134.
5 Kant, *The Critique of the Power Judgment* (5: 261), 144–5.
6 Kant, *The Critique of the Power of Judgment* (5: 261), 145.
7 Derrida, "Autoimmunity: Real and Symbolic Suicides," 90.
8 Derrida, "Autoimmunity: Real and Symbolic Suicides," 96–7.
9 Derrida, "Autoimmunity: Real and Symbolic Suicides," 97.
10 Derrida, "Politics and Friendship" in *Negotiations: Interventions and Interviews 1971–2001*, edited, translated and with an Introduction by Elizabeth Rottenberg, Stanford: Stanford University Press, 2002, 182.
11 F. Nietzsche, *On the Genealogy of Morals*, Book III, Section 11.
12 McCarthy, *No Country For Old Men*, London: Picador, 2005, 309.
13 John Cant also relates the fire in *The Road* to that described in *No Country for Old Men*, but suggests that in the latter case it signifies civilization being passed from father to son, while in the former it signifies "that vitality that burns within the ardent heart, the mystery that is the spark of life itself and that needs no reason to exist." *Cormac McCarthy and the Myth of American Exceptionalism*, New York and London: Routledge, 2008, 271.

9

Afterword: Acts of kindness— reflections on a different kind of road movie

MARY ZOURNAZI

One comes not into a world but into a question.[1]

"Walking into the darkness"

In February 2010, I went with some friends to see the movie *The Road* (dir. John Hillcoat, 2009) adapted from Cormac McCarthy's novel of the same name. It was early evening, the light outside was soft and almost translucent in its beauty, as we entered the cinema there was a dramatic shift from the soft light outside into the darkened cinema. As we sat down, the film's opening sequences gave us the full impact of the film and its visual aesthetics: low light and certain coldness that gives us the world as an uninhabitable place, but at the same time a strangely familiar world. *The Road* begins with an unspecified disaster that raises the concerns of the survival of a species, what it means to be human. Or put differently, why care about each other? Why care about the world in which we inhabit? For me, it signaled a different kind of road movie.

We need to differentiate *The Road* from post-apocalyptic as well as science fiction films, since it is attempting neither to escape nor to provide a future fantasy world of extremes. It is the world as it could be now. The film then is a film of *contemporaneity*. What we have is an "ecological road movie" so to speak, it is a film and story in a post-9/11 environment, it is an American story although its themes address a universal problem of personal and political conscience. Director John Hillcoat specifically worked to give the film certain "realism" in a surreal atmosphere and environment.[2] Hillcoat's realism is achieved through a cultural and visual memory, that is, familiar images that we have seen in different contexts for instance, the shopping trolley that the main characters cart around is a reminder of the homeless in every city. The costume and set design worked specifically to give an "aged" effect; the costumes were ill-fitted and found for the film to give the sense of the homeless characters as well as "homeless" wanderers in this hostile landscape.

The main characters of the "man" and "boy" are themselves home-less in this world environment just as they evoke familiarity and inti-macy that we share as humans. The father and son are cast to evoke the "everyman" or the every person, since it is Viggo Mortensen and Kodi Smit-McPhee's faces that can convey emotional range of every-day experience, that is, fear and survival as well as intimacy and love. The uncanny sense of the familiar world of the road also comes from real life news footage; for instance, the smoke stacks from 9/11 are used repeatedly in the background of scenes as well as images from natural disasters such as Hurricane Katrina and the volcanic eruption of Mount St Helens and its surrounds. Some of film locations were shot around areas impacted by Katrina such as Louisiana as well as Lake Erie that has been described by the author Margaret Atwood as:

Lake Erie — Big, flat, subject to unpredictable rages, and with dead spots in it — like Robert Mitchum's eyes. . .[3]

The film's visual code of little or no color contrast gives the film a desolate quality; the barren landscape resonates with the story's themes of human extremities and violence in a world destroyed. The set design and outside locations of the film move away from urban geography that is often the site of post-apocalyptic and science fiction films to give a feel for the road that is everywhere and nowhere. We get this feel through the wide angles of the film that give us the harshness of the road as well as the sense of a universality of place. By distilling the essential elements of McCarthy's book, the film focuses on the story at a human scale, to render visible the potential of humans and their vulnerability through the father and son as well as the violence of a world gone mad. Perhaps the main difference between the book and the film is that the book distills its language and is not driven by emotionality whereas the film uses sparse visual aesthetics while at the same time relying on drama to evoke fear, to demonstrate human's capacity for violence and cannibalism.

So what we face in the film is a dying world and social fabric, humans destroying each other and themselves in their fight for survival over diminishing resources. Since the human-made or natural disaster has already happened, the question that is put to us is: "what to do now?" Rather than try to resolve or blame the events that have already taken place, we are faced with the "here and now." In a literary sense, Dostoevsky already posed this ethical question in *Crime and Punishment* (1866), that is, how do we live with the consequences of a crime so to speak, and that is, the implications of the act that has already occurred, the murderous and selfish acts that we must live with. What Dostoevsky and the philosopher Emmanuel Levinas after him put to us is a question of responsibility, responsibility defined for all the world and humanity, as Dostoevsky states: "We are all responsible for all for all men before all, and I more than all the others."[4]

McCarthy's ethical concerns as they are brought to the screen, that is, "what to do now," are enhanced by cinema as a medium. Since cinema makes us aware of time, the ethical choices that *The Road* puts to us, that is, what to do now and how do we act, exist in the "here and now" of the film and the events that unfold within it. It is the boy in the film who embodies these ethical questions; the boy brings to light the ethics of the book and the film's faithful rendition of it. Even more so, it is the child or the archetype of the child and his courage that offers the hope and potential for a human survival since there the child offers freshness to the world and its interrelationships as opposed to the effects of ideology and habit. It is in this way that the film offers much in its visual attempt to give a feel for this road as well as the ethical questions of "everyman" and the responsibility "for all for all men before all and I more than others."

Everyman

Coming out of the film my friends and I had to adjust ourselves from the visual aesthetics and grayness of *The Road* to the darkness of the surrounding street. While standing on the street corner and adjusting our senses a homeless man came up to us, he looked like he had just stepped out of the film. He was the "everyman" of the film so to speak. The man started to earnestly talk to us, he seemed to be some kind of preacher, none of us knew exactly how to respond to him since he was rambling and non sensical, but one of my friends with a certain grace and respect listened to this man and responded to him. My friend's response to this man and my lack of compassion reminded me of the words of Levinas who wrote that "kindness is the only morality."[5] In the dehumanized reality and lawless world of *The Road*, there is no sense of morality or kindness; however, it is the "boy" who opens out the potential space for kindness. The intimacy between the father and the son offers us a way of survival against the odds, but it is the child who offers the potential.

Historically, it is the child as Adam Phillips and Barbara Taylor have written that provides the means for "civilising" culture when the world of adults and reason has reached its end.[6] Moreover, they argue that after the two world wars of the twentieth century, it was the mother-child relations that have been scrutinized as well as valorized to civilize culture once again. But in the world of *The Road*, we are left throughout most of the film with only the father and the child. The child is literally born out of despair since the mother does not want to give birth to this child in such a violent environment. What the mother represents as an archetype of care and creation no longer exists in this uninhabitable world. The mother inhabits only the space of memory in the film. And so, it is the child who can enable a new type of renewal and birth. The man's voice over at the start of the film suggests that the child is the "spirit" of life:

"If he is not the word of god, then god never spoke."

In the film, the child acts as the creative potential for the future through his very embodiment as well signaling how and what humanity might become. As Levinas writes, "The relation with the child — that is, the relation with the other that is not a power, but fecundity — establishes relationship with the absolute future, or infinite time."[7] The mother figure as a source of hope and renewal returns in the latter part of film as the reminder of the world's matrix, I will return to this point. Kindness is not about acts of heroism nor it is about the denial of events that are unspeakable, but is the only response that enables life and its affirmation. For instance, toward the end of the film, the man and the boy reach the coast with their shopping trolley of worldly possessions. While the father leaves the child and is searching the leftover goods from a shipwreck, his son weakened from the travel and the road falls asleep on the sand. The sleeping child is robbed of everything they possess.

In the next sequence, we come across the thief—who is an outcast from one of the communes—his body sullen and filthy, the thief in his destitution raises the stakes of what the everyman might imply in the film. The following film dialogue encapsulates the kindness that I am thinking of in the light of Levinas, and Phillips and Taylor:

Boy: Papa, Please don't kill the man.
Thief: Alright. (Drops knife)
    I done what you say.
    Listen to the boy.
Man: You've been following us?
    How long?
Thief: I aint fucken following you.
    I just saw the cart in the sand. I took it.
    That's all.
Man: Take off your clothes
    Take off your clothes. Every goddamn stitch of it.
Boy: No.
Thief: Alright. Fine.
    Take it easy.
Man: I'll kill you.
    Right where you stand.
Thief: Please, Mister.
    You aint got to do this.
Man: And the shoes.
    Throw them in the cart.
    Throw them in the cart.
    Do it!

Thief: You aint got to do this to me.
          You aint got to do me like this.
          I'm begging, please.
Boy: Papa!
Thief: I'll die out there.
Man: I leave you just the way you left us.
(Turns to the boy)
Help me pull the cart.

. . .

Man: Will you stop sulking.
          He's gone.
Boy: He's not gone
Man: What do you want me to do?
Boy: Just help him, Papa.
          Just help him.
          He's hungry.
          He's going to die.
Man: He's going to die anyway.
Boy: He's scared.
Man: I'm sacred. You understand?
          You're not the one who has to worry about everything.
Boy: [mumbles]
Man: What?
          What'd you say?
Child: Yes, I am.
          I AM ON THE ONE
Man: Ok.
          Help me push the cart.

(The boy returns the thief's clothes and leaves food for him by the side of the road.)

Phillips and Taylor argue that kindness involves "surviving hatred" to a certain degree, and it is the destitution and vulnerability of the other that stands before us that open the path to help, to be kind. Insights of philosophy and psychoanalysis on this point suggest that kindness involves ambivalence, but a healthy ambivalence. Freud and Winnicott offer some ways of considering this approach to kindness[8]:

For Winnicott, following Freud, the project with regard to kindness is to describe those forms of kindness that are not obstacles to the satisfactions of intimacy. It is as though, the psychoanalysts are saying, we have got our kindness wrong, that the ways in which we have described what we have in common, what holds us together, what keeps us keen on each other, have actually precluded us being together. That the kindnesses we have inherited are unsuited to modern world, have even in fact — in their most sentimentalized versions — become estrangement techniques. Love freed from hatred kills fellow feeling. If there is a kindness instinct it is going to have to take on board ambivalence in human relations. It is kind to be able to bear conflict, in oneself and others; it is kind, to oneself and others, to forego magic and sentimentality for reality. It is kind to see individuals as they are, rather than how we might want them to be; it is kind to care for people just as we find them.[9]

We might also be instructed by Vasily Grossman's book, *Life and Fate*,[10] which speaks of kindness and morality; the book is based on the battle for Stalingrad that documents both Stalin and Hilterian violence as well as anti-Semitism. For Grossman, kindness is the only path to freedom; but it is a kindness that may go "unwitnessed" since it emerges out of the everyday and responses to a given event or situation. Grossman's character Ikonnikov in the book documents "everyman," and this everyman's thoughts on kindness:

There exists, side by side with so terrible greater good, human kindness in everyday life. It is the kindness of the old lady who gives a piece of bread to a convict along the roadside. It is the kindness of a solider who holds his canteen out to a wounded enemy. The kindness of youth taking pity on old age, the kindness of a peasant who hides an old Jew in his barn. It is the kindness of those prison guards who risk their own freedom, smuggle the letters of prisoners out to wives and mothers. That private goodness of an individual for another individual is a goodness without witnesses, a little goodness without ideology. It could be called goodness without thought. The goodness of men outside the religious or social good.

That goodness has no discourse and no meaning. It is instinctive and blind. . .

The history of man is the struggle of evil trying to crush the tiny seed of humanity. But if even now the human has not been killed in man, evil will never prevail.[11]

. . .

But if we think about it, we realize that this private, senseless, incidental kindness is in fact eternal. It is extended to everything living, even to a mouse, even to a bent branch that a man straightens as he walks by.[12]

Carrying the fire

What made my friend's response to the homeless man remain so vivid in my imagination is that my friend shared a moment of tenderness with this man that the rest of us couldn't give him, or didn't want to. Kindness is the only morality that can be possible between "man and man," as the philosopher Martin Buber might put it.[13] For Buber, all ethical response arises out of the materiality of the world and its conditions, that is, what arises "between man and man." It is in this sphere between humans and between humans and the world that opens the potential for a different kind of ethics, an ethics of kindness. For it is in the recognition of our destitution and vulnerability that we become fully human.

In the last scene of the film, we see the potential for this ethics in a holistic sense; after the death of the man, the child is left alone at the end of the road. He comes across a figure in the distance, "the veteran." Between the veteran and the boy there is ambivalence as well as the "kindness" that ensues, it opens out the ethical demand and response between "man and man"

> Veteran: Who was that man you were with?
>   Is that your father?
> Boy: Yes, He was my Papa.
> Veteran: Maybe you should come with me.
> Boy: You one of the good guys?
> Veteran: Yeah, I'm one of the good guys.
>   Why don't you put that pistol away?
> Boy: I'm not supposed to let anyone take it from me.
>   No matter what.

Veteran: I don't want your pistol. I just don't want you pointing it at me.

Listen you got two choices here: You can stay here with your Papa, or you can go with me. If you stay here you need to keep off the road.

Boy: How do I know you're one of the good guys?

Veteran: You don't. You'll just have to take a shot.

Boy: Do you have any kids?

Veteran: Yes we do.

Boy: Do you have a little boy?

Veteran: I have a little boy and a little girl.

Boy: How old is he?

Veteran: About your age. A little older.

Boy: So you didn't eat them?

Veteran: No.

Boy: You don't eat people?

Veteran: No. We don't eat people.

Boy: And are you carrying the fire?

Veteran: Am I what?

Boy: And are you carrying the fire?

Veteran: You're kind of weirded out, aren't you kid?

Boy: Well, are you?

Veteran: Yeah. I'm carrying the fire.

Boy: I can come with you?

Veteran: Yes, you can.

The child demonstrates a kind of altruism that Auguste Comte may have had in mind when he invented the term, that is, altruism is what propels humanity and its progress.[14] In some ways, altruism which is the extension of the kindness I refer to here can be thought of as an "inbuilt" human tendency. We might say then humans have this inbuilt capacity for altruism, the "origins of the species" so to speak is not inherently selfish and based on survival of the fittest above and beyond everyone and everything else, but built on a devotion *to* and regard *for* each other. Genuine care. In *The Road*, the child reminds us of this "instinct," this "kindness instinct" does not ignore nor refrain from the "real," that is, encounters that may be hostile or irrevocable, but rather kindness enables the affirmation of life and its continual renewal and hope.

Later, when the child is introduced to the veteran's wife and family, the woman gently caresses the boy's face. Here the mother returns as the matrix of the world just as the boy presents us with renewal and hope; the mother's archetypal qualities give us the creative and reproductive power of an enduring world, "for the maternal is always that which is already there."[15] It is in this moment too we are reminded that there are others in the world who choose a different ethical path than the one's taken by the bands of mercenaries and cannibals in the film. In an ecological sense, the film gives us the awareness that life is deeply social. It displays a kind of tenderness in the midst of brutality, a hope of a material kind.

To end, the last words from McCarthy's novel as well as the atmosphere given in the last moments of the film surmise the visual poetry of kindness in an unkind world. It reminds us of the everyday, infinity and life's mystery:

> The woman when she saw him put her arms around him and held him. Oh, she said, I am so glad to see you. She would talk to him sometimes about God. He tried to talk to God but the best thing was to talk to his father and he did talk to him and he didnt forget. The woman said that was all right. She said that the breath of God was his breath yet though it pass from man to man through all of time.
>
> Once there were brook trout in the streams in the mountains. You could see them standing in the amber current where the white edges of their fins wimpled softly in the flow. They smelled of moss in your hand. Polished and muscular and torsional. On their backs were vermiculate patterns that were maps of the world in its becoming. Maps and Mazes. Of a thing which could not be put back. Not be made right again. In the deep glens where they lived all things were older than man and they hummed of mystery. (306–7)

Notes

1   Emmanuel Levinas, "Ethics as First Philosophy," in *The Levinas Reader*, trans. Seán Hand and Michael Temple (Oxford: Basil Blackwell, 1989).

2 See Interview with John Hillcoat www.afi.org.u/AM/Content
   ManagerNet/HTMLDisplay.aspx?ContentID=9971&Section=The_
   Road_An_interview_with_director_John_Hillcoat (accessed 24
   October, 2011).

3 Margaret Atwood, "On Lake Erie's Demise" in www.thestar.com/
   SpecialSections/EarthHour/article/294693 (accessed 2 November,
   2011).

4 Emmanuel Levinas, "Responsibility For the Other," in *Ethics and
   Infinity*, trans. Richard A. Cohen (Pittsburgh: Duquesne University
   Press), 101.

5 See Emmanuel Levinas, "The Name of a Dog, or Natural Rights," in
   Difficult Freedom, trans. Seán Hand (Baltimore: The John Hopkins
   University Press, 1997), 151–3.

6 See Adam Phillips and Barbara Taylor, *On Kindness* (London:
   Penguin, 2009).

7 Emmanuel Levinas, *Totality and Infinity*, trans. Alphonso Lingis
   (Pittsburgh: Duquesne University Press), 268.

8 See D.W. Winnicott "Hate in Countertransference," in *Through
   Pediatrics to Psychoanalysis, Collected Papers* (London: Karnac
   Books, 2004 [1947]). Winnicott's later works on "holding" and
   ambivalence give the grounds for the kind of ethical space in which
   we can learn to "be"; the space of becoming real in our environment.

9 Phillips and Taylor, *On Kindness*, 95–6.

10 See Vasily Grossman, *Life and Fate — A Novel*, trans. Robert
   Chandler (London: Harvill, 1985).

11 Vasily Grossman, *Life and Fate,* cited in Emmanuel Levinas, "Beyond
   Memory" in In the Time of Nations, trans. Michael B. Smith
   (Bloomington and Indianapolis: Indiana University Press, 1994),
   90–91.

12 Grossman, *Life and Fate*, 408.

13 See Martin Buber, *Between Man and Man*, trans. Ronald Gregor-
   Smith (London and New York: Routledge, 2002 [1947]).

14 See Auguste Comte, *System of Positive Polity*, Third Volume (New
   York: Burt Franklin [1883] 1968).

15 Franz Rosenzweig writes of the maternal and its qualities are the
   basis of all creation. See Rosenzweig's *Star of Redemption*, trans.
   William W. Hallo (Notre Dame: University of Notre Dame Press,
   2002 [1921]), 159.

NOTES ON CONTRIBUTORS

Chris Danta is an ARC Postdoctoral Fellow in the School of English, Media and Performing Arts at the University of New South Wales. He is the author of *Literature Suspends Death: Sacrifice and Storytelling in Kierkegaard, Kafka and Blanchot* (Continuum, 2011) and the co-editor of *Strong Opinions: J.M. Coetzee and the Authority of Contemporary Fiction* (Continuum, 2011).

Grace Hellyer is completing her doctorate at the University of New South Wales where she also teaches undergraduate courses on the history of the novel. Her research explores the relationship between the nineteenth-century American Gothic and the emergence of democratic government. She has recently addressed international conferences in Australia and the UK, speaking on the allegorical mode in literature.

Julian Murphet is Professor in Modern Film and Literature, Convenor of the Disciplines of English and Film, and Director of the Centre for Modernism Studies in Australia, at the University of New South Wales. He has published *Literature and Race in Los Angeles* and *Multimedia Modernism*, as well as numerous articles and chapters on a range of modern and contemporary cultural matters.

Paul Patton is Professor of Philosophy at the University of New South Wales. His recent publications include *Deleuzian Concepts: Philosophy, Colonization, Politics* (Stanford, 2010) as well as the edited collections *Deleuze and the Postcolonial* (Edinburgh, 2010) and *Poetics of In-Between Space* (Pusan National UP, 2005). With Continuum he has published a translation of Deleuze's *Difference* *and Repetition* (2004) and the co-edited collection, *Between Deleuze and Derrida* (2003). Patton's work has appeared in major journals and collections, and has been translated into multiple languages.

Sean Pryor lectures in English at the University of New South Wales. He is the author of *W. B. Yeats, Ezra Pound and the Poetry of Paradise* (Ashgate, 2011), and is currently working on the sense of fallenness in twentieth-century poetry.

Paul Sheehan is a Senior Lecturer in the Department of English at Macquarie University, Sydney, Australia. He is the author of *Modernism, Narrative and Humanism* (Cambridge UP, 2002) and the editor of *Becoming Human: New Perspectives on the Inhuman Condition* (Praeger, 2003). Most recently, he has completed a historical poetics of violence and aesthetics in the literature and film of the last century, and has published essays on screen animals (in *SubStance*), Samuel Beckett (*Samuel Beckett Today*), and J. M. Coetzee (*Twentieth Century Fiction*).

Mark Steven is a graduate student at the University of Sydney, where he teaches media, popular culture, and cultural theory. He has published articles and chapters on literature, cinema, and philosophy, and is soon to commence doctoral research on modernist poetics.

Mary Zournazi teaches at the University of New South Wales. She is the author of several books including *Hope—New Philosophies for Change* (Routledge, 2003), *Keywords to War* (Scribe, 2007) and forthcoming with the filmmaker Wim Wenders, *Inventing Peace*.

INDEX

Printed in Poland
by Amazon Fulfillment
Poland Sp. z o.o., Wrocław